T9597-AA-RPT-010/SUPSALV

0910-LP-140-9100

SPACE SHUTTLE CHALLENGER SALVAGE REPORT

THIS DOCUMENT HAS BEEN APPROVED FOR PUBLIC RELEASE AND SALE;
ITS DISTRIBUTION IS UNLIMITED.

PUBLISHED BY DIRECTION OF COMMANDER, NAVAL SEA SYSTEMS COMMAND

29 APRIL 1988

SUPERVISOR OF SALVAGE
U.S. NAVY

29 April 1988

FOREWORD

The search and salvage of the space shuttle CHALLENGER from February through August 1986 was the largest such operation ever conducted by the U.S. Navy. Several thousand people, numerous surface vessels, a nuclear-powered research submarine and several unmanned and manned submersibles played major roles in the successful underwater search and object recovery operation.

This report examines the underwater search and salvage of the CHALLENGER from the command and management, as well as technical perspectives. Lessons learned were derived from an operation which demanded coordination of diverse assets from multiple sources to meet the salvage objectives.

For all its successes, the CHALLENGER salvage mission illustrated the continued validity of some lessons the Navy has learned over many years of undersea work. Parts of this report's message will have direct application to some but only general interest to others. We have prepared this report to enable future salvage officers and engineers to gain some lasting value from what otherwise was a national loss.

C. A. Bartholomew
Captain, USN

TABLE OF CONTENTS

	PAGE
CHAPTER 1 - INTRODUCTION AND BACKGROUND SUMMARY	2
1.1 SUPSALV Tasking	2
1.2 Scope of SUPSALV Mission	2
1.3 Purpose of Report	2
1.4 SUPSALV Authority	6
1.5 Involvement with NASA	6
1.5.1 SRB Recovery	6
1.5.2 STS-4 Search and Salvage	6
1.6 Delta Rocket Recovery	6
CHAPTER 2 - COMMAND AND ORGANIZATION	9
2.1 Establishing Command	9
2.2 Immediate Response	9
2.3 Transition to SUPSALV	9
2.4 NASA Search, Recovery and Reconstruction Team	9
2.5 Organization of Underwater Search and Salvage Operations	11
2.6 Supporting Forces	11
2.6.1 Ships	11
2.6.2 Other Navy Units	11
2.6.3 U. S. Coast Guard	11
2.6.4 Naval Eastern Oceanographic Center, Norfolk, VA	11
2.6.5 Contractors	13
CHAPTER 3 - PLANNING, LOGISTICS AND MANAGEMENT	15
3.1 STS 51-L Operations Plan	15
3.2 Search	15
3.2.1 Ship Movements	15
3.2.2 Prioritization	15
3.2.3 Current	15
3.2.4 Contact Database	15
3.3 Object Classification	16
3.4 Contact Subclassification	16
3.5 Object Recovery Priority	16
3.6 Logistics	16
3.7 Shorebased Support	16
3.8 Mobilization	16
3.9 Navy Shorebased Command Post	17
3.10 Primary Assets	18
3.10.1 Navy Platforms	18
3.10.2 NASA Platforms	18
3.10.3 USAF LCU	18
3.10.4 Commercial Platforms	18
3.10.5 Submersible Vehicles	19
3.11 Management	19
3.11.1 Information Flow	19
3.11.2 Daily Plan	21

TABLE OF CONTENTS (Continued)

		PAGE
3.12 Public Affairs		21
3.13 Financial Management		22

CHAPTER 4 - THE SEARCH — 24
- 4.1 Search Area — 24
  - 4.1.1 Initial Search Area — 24
  - 4.1.2 Expanded Search Area — 24
  - 4.1.3 Search Completion — 24
- 4.2 Contact Summary — 24
- 4.3 Selection of Assets - Search Operations — 27
  - 4.3.1 Search Platforms — 27
  - 4.3.2 NR-1 — 27
  - 4.3.3 Navigation Systems — 28
  - 4.3.4 Search Equipment — 28
- 4.4 Sonar Search Techniques — 29
  - 4.4.1 Line Pattern — 29
  - 4.4.2 Search Data Processing — 29
  - 4.4.3 Contact Priority — 30
  - 4.4.4 High Resolution Sonar — 30
- 4.5 Final Search Results — 30

CHAPTER 5 - CLASSIFICATION AND RECOVERY OF SOLID ROCKET BOOSTERS — 32
- 5.1 SRB Configuration — 32
- 5.2 Distribution of SRB Debris — 32
- 5.3 SRB Classification — 32
  - 5.3.1 NR-1 Classification Operations — 37
- 5.4 Use of Recovery Assets — 37
  - 5.4.1 Heavy Lift Vessels — 37
  - 5.4.2 Remotely Operated Vehicles (ROV's) — 37
  - 5.4.3 Manned Submersibles — 37
  - 5.4.4 Attachment Tools — 37
- 5.5 Recovery Methods — 39
- 5.6 Safety and Hazards — 40
  - 5.6.1 Ordnance — 40
  - 5.6.2 Propellant — 42
- 5.7 STENA WORKHORSE SRB Recovery — 42
- 5.8 Submarine Rescue Ship SRB Recovery — 42
- 5.9 Recovery of the Right SRB Critical Joint — 42
- 5.10 Completion of SRB Recovery Operations — 44
- 5.11 SRB Recovery Summary — 44

CHAPTER 6 - CLASSIFICATION AND RECOVERY OF ORBITER AND PAYLOAD — 51
- 6.1 Classification and Recovery — 51
  - 6.1.2 Initial Recovery — 51
  - 6.1.3 Crew Compartment — 51
- 6.2 Extended Operations — 53

TABLE OF CONTENTS (Concluded)

		PAGE
6.3	Recovery Methods	53
6.3.1	Divers	53
6.3.2	Combined Jack-stay Search Method	56
6.3.3	Standard Jack-stay Search Method	57
6.3.4	ROV's and Submersibles	57
6.4	Final Contact Statistics	58

CHAPTER 7 - LESSONS LEARNED — 60
- 7.1 Command and Control — 60
- 7.2 Public Affairs — 60
- 7.3 Navigational Accuracy of Designated Sonar Contacts — 60
- 7.4 Submarine NR-1 Utilization — 61
  - 7.4.1 Navigational Accuracy — 61
  - 7.4.2 Water Management — 61
- 7.5 Metal Detectors — 62
- 7.6 ROV's Versus Manned Submersibles — 62
- 7.7 Dynamic Positioning — 63
- 7.8 Sonar for Direct Diver Support — 63

CHAPTER 8 - CONCLUSIONS — 65

REFERENCES — 66

APPENDICES

A	NAVAL MESSAGES	A-1
B	MAJOR MOBILIZED ASSETS	B-1
C	CONTACTS RECOVERED	C-1

Challenger Report

List of Exhibits

No.	Title	Page
1	STS 51-L at Dawn Prior to Liftoff	1
2	STS 51-L Flight Trajectory and Impact	3
3	Summary Statistics of Challenger Salvage	4
4	Major Events During Operation	5
5	SUPSALV Command Management Briefing	8
6	STS 51-L Design Analysis Force Organization	10
7	STS 51-L Search, Recovery and Reconstruction Team	10
8	Navy Organization for Underwater Salvage Operation	12
9	Navy Shore Command Complex	14
10	Major Deployed Assets	17
11	Daily Information Flow	20
12	Final Search Area	23
13	Distribution of 881 Designated Sonar Contacts	25
14	G.W. PIERCE	26
15	Arrangement of Typical SRB	31
16	SRB Joint Configuration and Nomenclature	33
17	SRB and Orbiter Debris Areas	34
18	Distribution of SRB Contacts from Along the Failed Joint Circumference	35
19	NR-1 and Crew	36
20	STENA WORKHORSE Deploying GEMINI in Heavy Seas	38
21	STENA WORKHORSE and GEMINI Configuration	41
22	Propellant Burning from a Booster Piece	43
23	Contact #131 Interior and Exterior Surfaces	45

Challenger Report

List of Exhibits (Concluded)

No.	Title	Page
24	Contact #131 Recovery Right SRB	46
25	Contact #712 Interior and Exterior Surfaces	47
26	Composite of Right SRB Debris Aft Segment	48
27	Full-size Styrofoam Composite of Major Pieces Recovered from Right SRB	49
28	Arrangement of the Orbiter and Related Components	50
29	Western Edge of the Search Area	52
30	Shallow Water Search Area	54
31	Preparing to Dive from the PRESERVER	55
32	Combined Jack-stay and Circle Method	56
33	Jack-stay Search Method	57
34	Press Conference	59
35	CHALLENGER Liftoff	64

Chapter 1
INTRODUCTION AND BACKGROUND SUMMARY

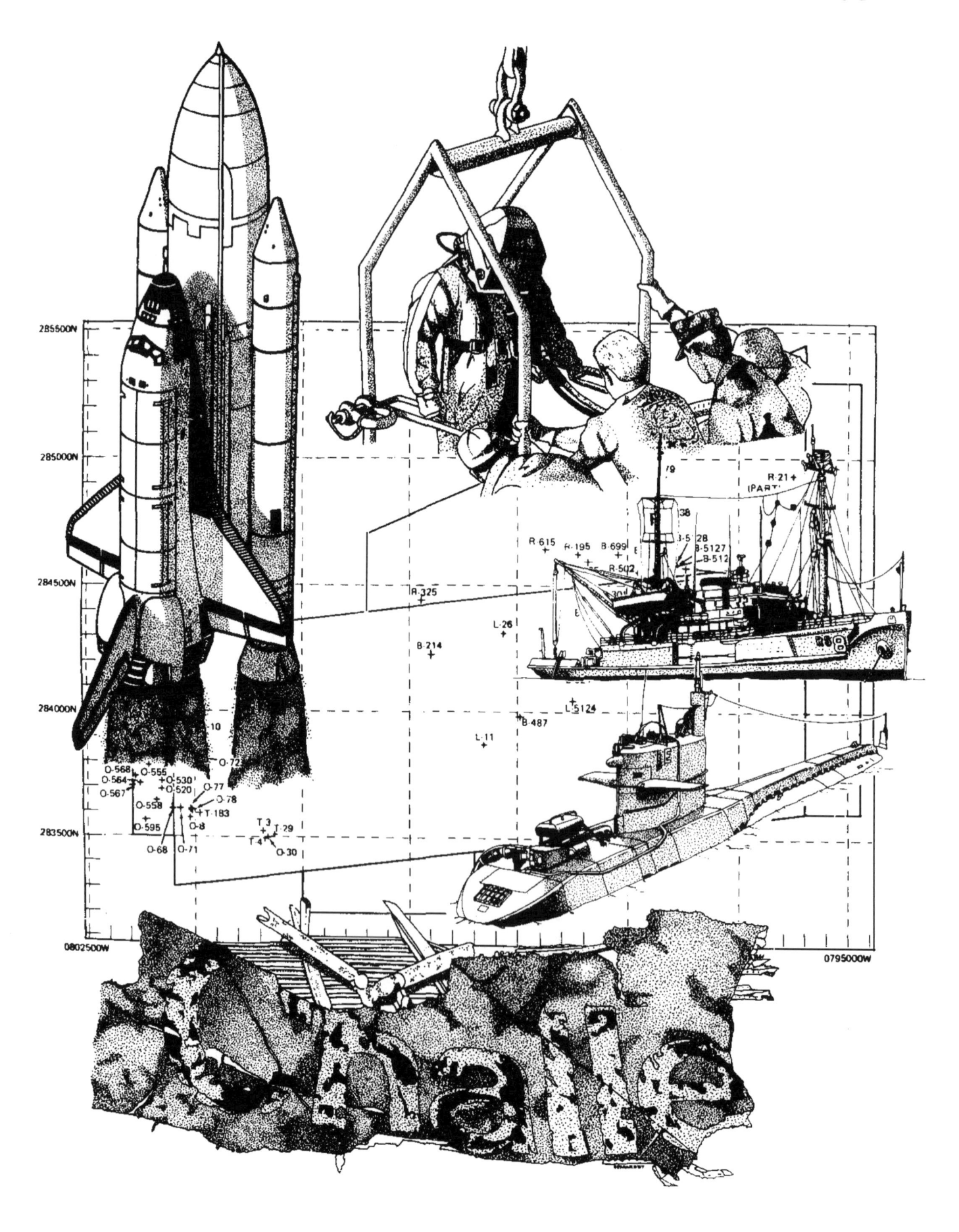

Exhibit 1. STS 51-L at Dawn Prior to Liftoff

Chapter 1
INTRODUCTION AND BACKGROUND SUMMARY

At 1130 Eastern Standard Time on 28 January 1986, the space shuttle CHALLENGER, Space Transportation System (STS) Mission 51-L (Exhibit 1), was launched from Pad 39B of the John F. Kennedy Space Center (KSC), Cape Canaveral, Florida. Seventy-three seconds later the spacecraft exploded in flight over the Atlantic Ocean east-northeast of KSC (Exhibit 2).

1.1 SUPSALV Tasking. On 31 January, the U.S. Navy Supervisor of Salvage (SUPSALV) was tasked to salvage CHALLENGER. The Commander-in-Chief, U.S. Atlantic Fleet (CINCLANTFLT) was tasked to provide support. The specified missions were recovery of:

(1) Debris to determine cause of accident
(2) Crew compartment for humanitarian reasons
(3) All hazardous components
(4) Selected payload components
(5) Spacecraft structure to help ascertain vehicle breakup mode.

The operation under the Supervisor of Salvage (SUPSALV) officially commenced 8 February 1986. The scope of this search and salvage mission became the largest ever undertaken in terms of geographic area, weight and number of individual pieces salvaged. It successfully concluded on 29 August 1986.

1.2 Scope of SUPSALV Mission. For seven months SUPSALV directed an operation which systematically inspected in excess of 486 square nautical miles (sq nm) of ocean floor in water depths ranging from 10 to well in excess of 1,200 feet of seawater (fsw). Of a total of 711 sonar contacts visually classified, 187 confirmed STS 51-L related pieces were located and 167 recovered. Several thousand people, sixteen surface vessels, a nuclear-powered research submarine and several unmanned and manned submersibles played roles in the operation. Exhibit 3 summarizes the statistics of the effort and Exhibit 4 gives a chronology of major events in the operation.

1.3 Purpose of Report. This report discusses the command, management and technical efforts of the search and salvage operation. As with any large operation, many situational constraints guided the mission. For example the operation was strongly influenced by environmental factors such as surface currents of up to five knots (kts) from the Gulf Stream, frequent weather fronts producing high winds and rough seas and water depths which exceeded 1200 fsw. Dealing with the combined effects of these natural phenomena required the selection and use of both conventional and specialized assets. Other operational factors included:

1. Number and haphazard dispersal of objects from the explosion which were mingled with numerous extraneous objects on the ocean floor

2. Coordination of command and authority among multiple organizations including U. S. Navy (USN), National Aeronautics and Space Administration (NASA), Department of Defense Manager for Space Transportation System Contingency Support Operations (DDMS), U.S Air Force (USAF), U. S. Coast Guard (USCG), major contractors and subcontractors

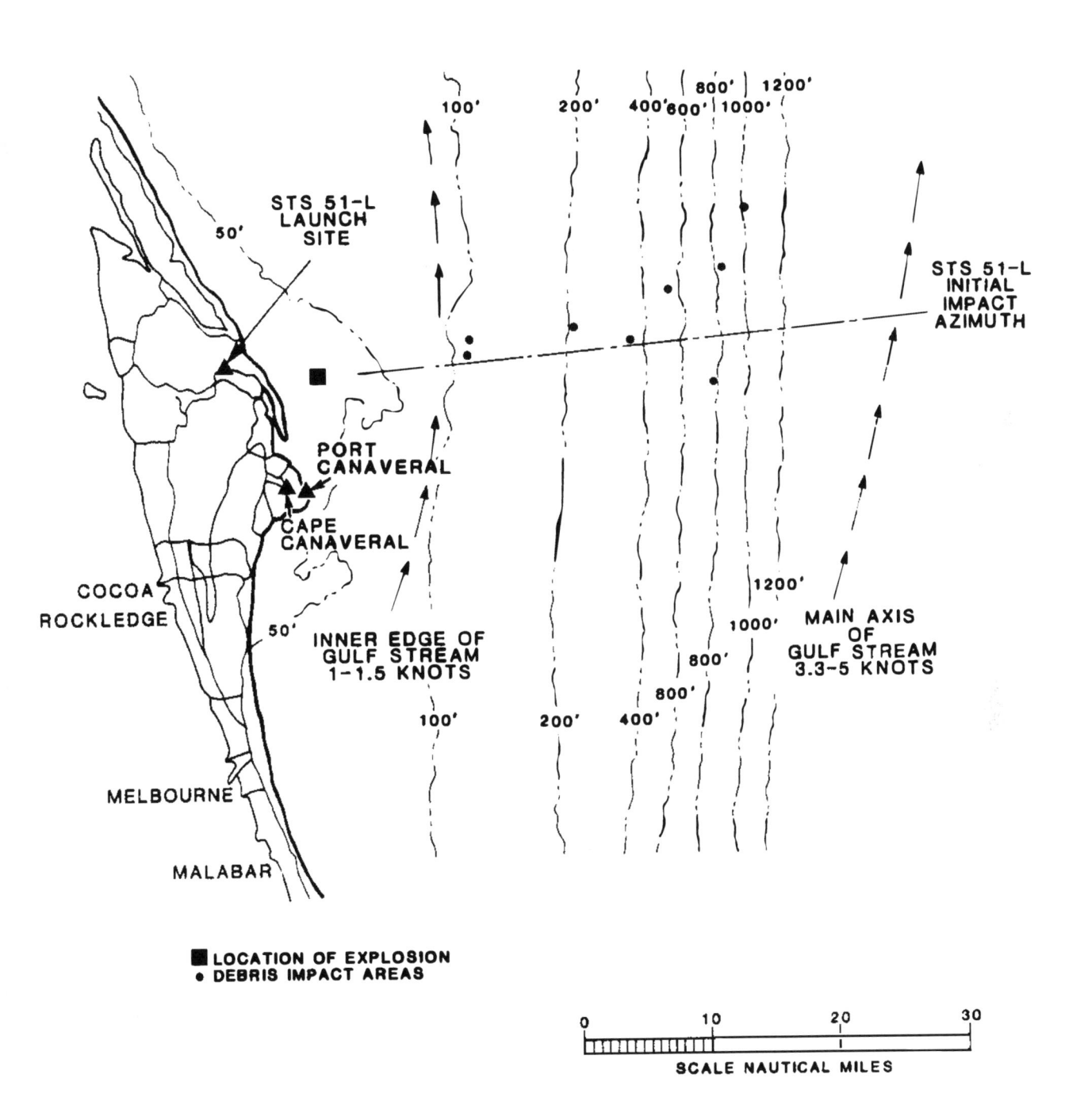

Exhibit 2. STS 51-L Flight Trajectory and Impact

Exhibit 3
Summary Statistics of CHALLENGER Salvage

- 16 surface ships (1,161 ship days)
  - 4 USN
  - 3 NASA
  - 1 USAF
  - 8 Contract

- 8 Multiuser navigation systems

- 6 Side scan sonar systems

- 9,660 nm of sonar search lines generating 38,400 ft. of sonar traces

- 881 sonar contacts designated

- 711 sonar contacts investigated

- 4 ROV's, 457 dives with 1,435 operational hours underwater

- 2 manned submersibles, 104 dives for 296 hours

- Submarine NR-1, 4 missions with 744 hours bottom time

- Divers conducted 3,077 dives with 1,549 hours bottom time

- 118 tons of debris recovered from 167 confirmed STS 51-L contacts

Exhibit 4
Major Events During Operation

28 Jan	•	STS 51-L launch and failure
	•	DDMS initiates surface Search and Recovery (SAR) operations under USCG direction
31 Jan	•	DDMS officially tasks NAVSEA through CNO to command underwater search operations
6 Feb	•	USS PRESERVER (ARS 8) arrives Port Canaveral (first U.S. Navy ship on scene in support of underwater Salvage Operations)
8 Feb	•	Underwater salvage operations officially commence
22 Feb	•	SEA-LINK II submersible confirms right SRB debris at Contact #21
	•	Search area expanded from initial 250 to 370 sq nm; area progressively expanded to 486 sq nm
1 Mar	•	Deep salvage ship STENA WORKHORSE with ROV GEMINI installed arrives in search area
	•	LIBERTY STAR locates Contact #131 (upper portion of right SRB with burn hole)
7 Mar	•	USAF LCU identifies crew compartment
8 Mar	•	Crew compartment confirmed by PRESERVER; salvage commences
1 Apr	•	Four search ships complete large area side scan sonar search
11 Apr	•	USS PRESERVER departs Port Canaveral having been relieved by USS OPPORTUNE (ARS 41)
12 Apr	•	Submarine NR-1 completes 13-day mission which classifies 281 sonar contacts of which 22 are SRB related
13 Apr	•	Contact #131 recovered
26 Apr	•	Contact #712, lower portion of right SRB burn hole, recovered
29 Apr	•	All NASA-specified recoveries from deep water completed; STENA WORKHORSE, GEMINI, and SEA-LINK submersibles released; shallow water operations continue for Orbiter and payload recovery
1 Jun	•	USS OPPORTUNE departs Port Canaveral ending USN ship presence
29 Aug	•	Mission concludes; all remaining assets and Navy Command van complex demobilized
26 Sep	•	Final NAVSEA report submitted to NASA.

3. High level of public and media interest which required constant care and attention to ensure the proper flow of information and personnel access to the area and facilities

4. Need to quickly locate and recover critical pieces of the solid rocket boosters (SRB's) and shuttle compartment to satisfy the requirements of NASA and the Presidential Commission charged to investigate the accident.

The loss of CHALLENGER provided the Navy diving and salvage community with valuable lessons and experience. A summary of the important lessons learned is contained in Chapter 7 of this report.

1.4 SUPSALV Authority. SUPSALV supports the Fleet from his staff role (Code OOC) to the Commander, Naval Sea Systems Command (NAVSEA) in Washington, D.C. SUPSALV has several distinct responsibilities such as providing technical support to the Fleet in the areas of salvage, diving, underwater ship husbandry, oil and hazardous materials spill response and ocean engineering. In addition SUPSALV has operational responsibilities and the capability to augment Fleet diving and salvage units. SUPSALV maintains contracts with commercial salvors worldwide to provide emergency salvage services to the Fleet, other government agencies, foreign governments through the U.S. Department of State and, under certain circumstances to the private sector.

1.5 Involvement with NASA. The Navy and NASA have cooperated closely since the inception of the manned space program in the 1960's. In the early days of the space program, the Navy provided search and rescue support to recover astronauts and space capsules from the open sea.

1.5.1 SRB Recovery. As the space shuttle program evolved and the reusable SRB concept was adopted, SUPSALV provided technical advice and training to NASA in developing recovery techniques for the expended SRB's. As a result, NASA developed its own capability to recover floating boosters using two specially built support ships. Contingency plans have been developed jointly for Navy support in the event of NASA system failures.

1.5.2 STS-4 Search and Salvage. In July of 1982 a parachute-related malfunction during the launch of the Space Shuttle Mission STS-4 caused two SRB's to sink in 3,200 fsw approximately 140 miles east of KSC. NASA requested SUPSALV assistance to salvage the boosters. The commercial ROV SCARAB was utilized to survey the site. Photographs taken by SCARAB revealed that damage to the SRB's was extensive. While preparing for the heavy lift salvage of one of the boosters, several attempts were made to recover parachutes using the SCARAB and a lift line deployed from the USNS POWHATAN (T-ATF 166). Bottom currents of approximately three knots prevented hookup after extensive ROV operations. However, because the cause of the malfunction was subsequently determined by NASA from review of the SCARAB videotapes, little additional information was judged to be gained from a difficult and expensive salvage of the SRB's or the parachutes. The salvage operation was therefore terminated.

1.6 Delta Rocket Recovery. On 3 May 1986 during the STS 51-L recovery operations a Delta rocket with a GOES-G satellite payload was launched from Cape Canaveral Air Force Station (AFS). The rocket experienced a main engine shutdown 71 seconds into the flight and the Range Safety Officer initiated the destruct sequence. The impact area of the Delta launch was south of the STS 51-L search area. SUPSALV was tasked to search and salvage portions of the rocket. Several of the assets being used for the STS 51-L salvage were diverted to the impact area to perform the search and recovery. Details of this operation, which are hardly more than a small subset of the CHALLENGER operation, are not included in this report.

Chapter 2
COMMAND AND ORGANIZATION

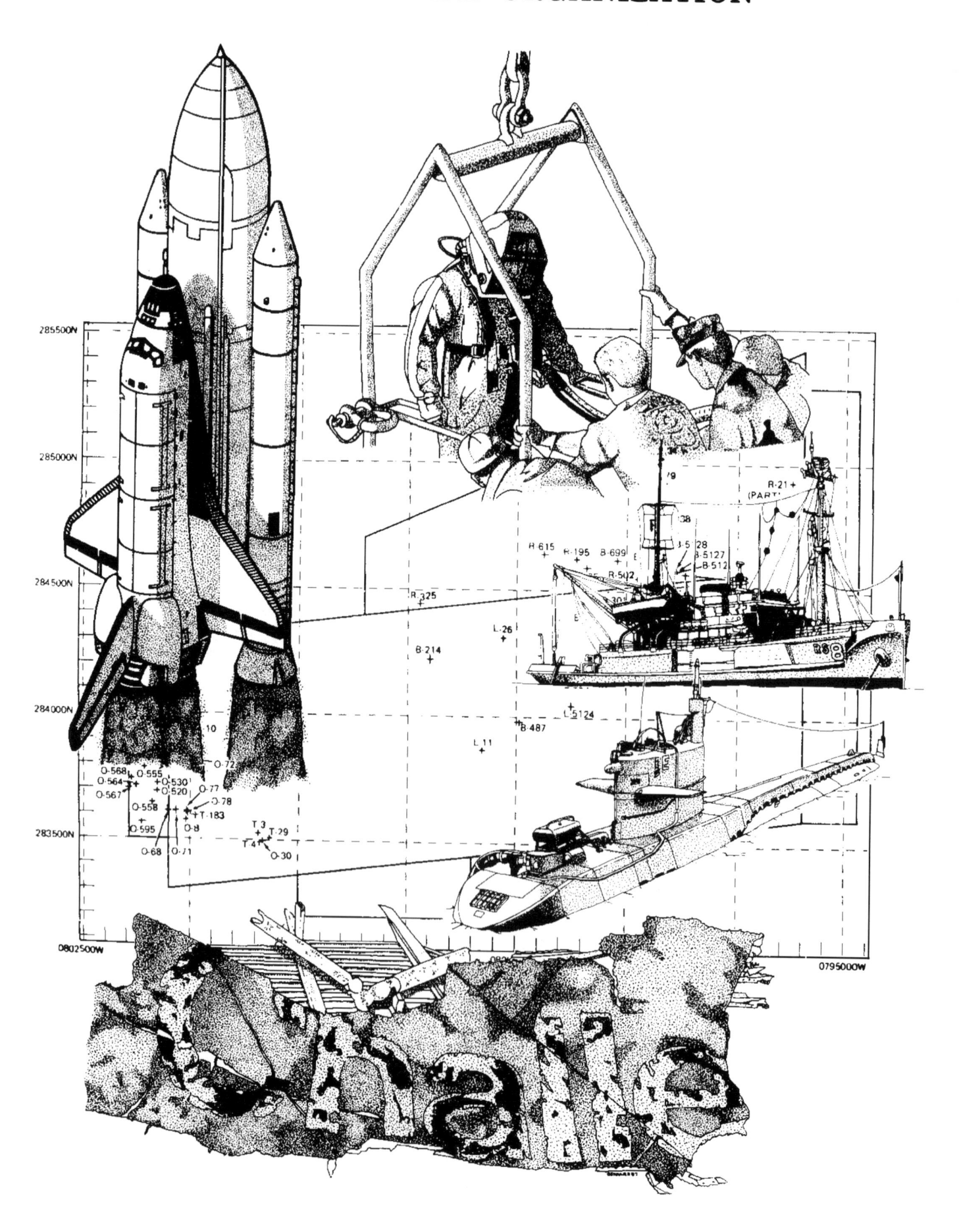

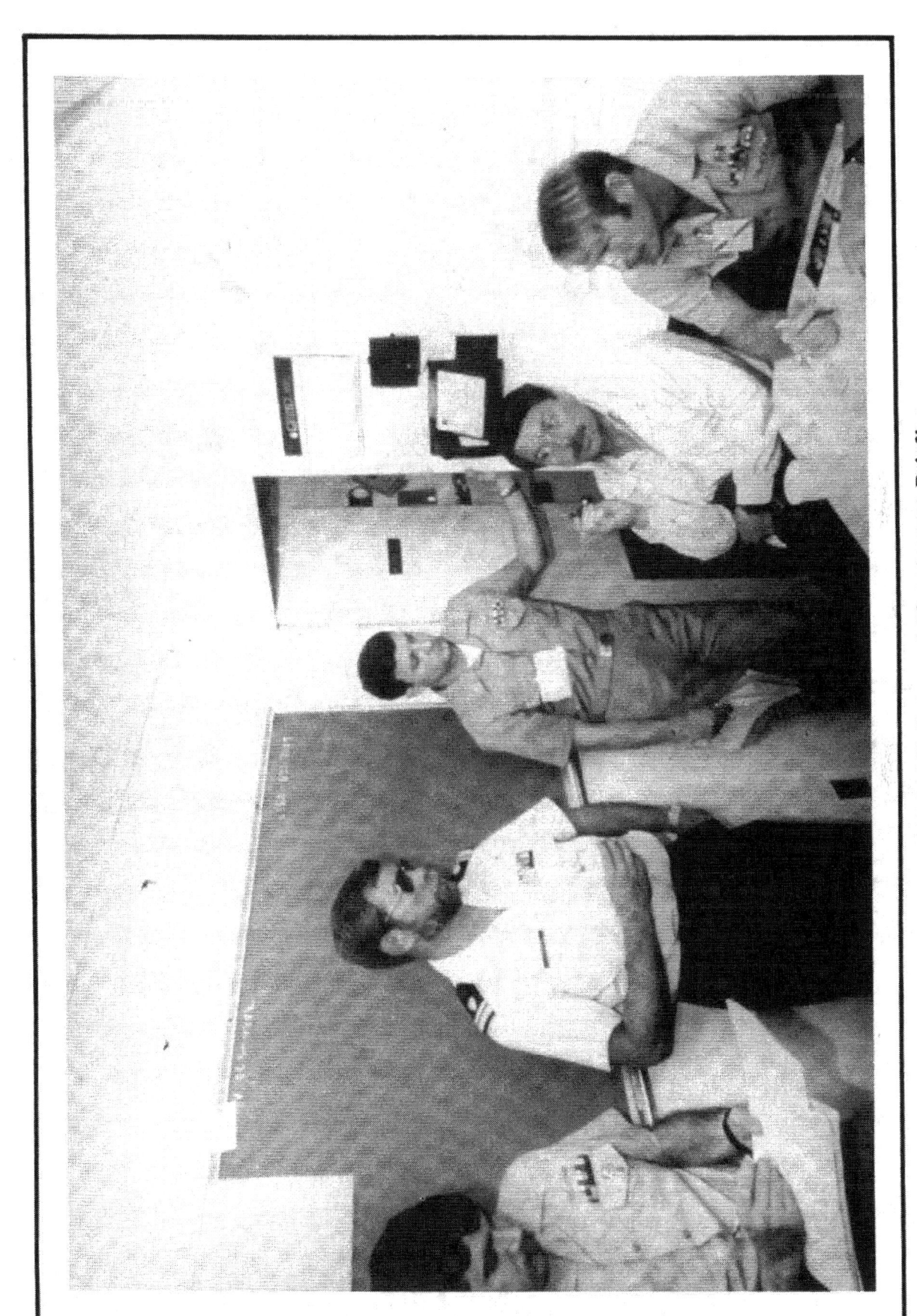

Exhibit 5. SUPSALV Command Management Briefing

Chapter 2
COMMAND AND ORGANIZATION

At the direction of the Chief of Naval Operations (CNO), SUPSALV on 8 February 1986 assumed operational control (Exhibit 5) of U.S. Navy, NASA, USAF, USCG and Navy contractor assets assigned to conduct the CHALLENGER STS 51-L search and salvage. Although the scale of operations in the STS 51-L recovery was larger than any previous SUPSALV underwater operations, it did not substantially alter established command relationships. The command organization and resulting authority over day-to-day efforts was particularly important to the success of this operation because of its large scope. Exhibits 6, 7, and 8 depict the overall command organization and interrelationships among key elements of the operation at the Presidential Task Force, NASA reconstruction, and underwater salvage operations levels respectively.

2.1 Establishing Command. The KSC Support Operations Center notified the National Military Command Center (NMCC) in Washington, D.C. of the CHALLENGER's loss within two minutes. The Joint Chiefs of Staff (JCS) established a Shuttle Response Cell. This immediate involvement of the Department of Defense (DoD) was enabled by the DoD Manager for Space Transportation System Contingency Support Operations (DDMS) which serves as the working interface between the DoD and NASA. The DoD Manager, a USAF general officer, provides access for priority requirements to the Office of the Secretary of Defense (OSD) through JCS (code J3). DDMS also provides management and control over DoD support forces, facilities and assets that are committed to contingency operations.

2.2 Immediate Response. DDMS simultaneously initiated a surface search and rescue operation under the NASA Launch Recovery Director (LRD) in accordance with the STS Contingency Support Operations Plan of 1 December 1985. The surface search was coordinated by the USCG with assistance from six USN ships and the Air Force Eastern Space and Missile Center (ESMC).

2.3 Transition to SUPSALV. Five hours after the mishap, DDMS alerted SUPSALV and asked that a representative be sent to Cape Canaveral AFS. Subsequent to a briefing by Dr. Dale Uhler, Deputy SUPSALV, who outlined the Navy's preliminary plan of action, DDMS requested that the Navy undertake the STS 51-L underwater search and salvage mission. CNO tasked NAVSEA accordingly and requested that CINCLANTFLT provide support as needed. Tasking messages are shown in Appendix A, Exhibits A-1 and A-2.

2.4 NASA Search, Recovery and Reconstruction Team. On 29 January 1986, Dr. William Graham, NASA's Acting Administrator, appointed Mr. Jesse Moore to act as the Chairman of the interim STS 51-L Mishap Investigation Board. Mr. Moore requested that USAF Col. Edward O'Connor coordinate the search and recovery organizations for recovery of the flight components which would provide the basis for the accident investigation. Col. O'Connor provided direction and operational control to the NASA reconstruction effort until formally chartered as Team Leader for the Search, Recovery and Reconstruction Team on 20 March 1986. The data and Design Analysis Task Force was organized as shown in Exhibit 6. The Search, Recovery and Reconstruction Team, a major element of the Task Force, is shown in Exhibit 7.

```
                    ┌─────────────────────────┐
                    │ RADM RICHARD TRULY      │──────┐  ┌──────────────┐
                    │      CHAIRMAN           │      ├──│ STAFF (HQS)  │
                    ├─────────────────────────┤      │  └──────────────┘
                    │ JAMES R. THOMPSON, JR   │      │  ┌──────────────┐
                    │    VICE CHAIRMAN        │──────┴──│ STAFF (KSC)  │
                    └─────────────────────────┘         └──────────────┘
```

| PROJECT ANALYSIS TEAM | LAUNCH SYSTEM PROCESSING ANALYSIS TEAM | ACCIDENT ANALYSIS TEAM | MISSION OPERATIONS ANALYSIS TEAM |

| SEARCH, RECOVERY AND RECONSTRUCTION TEAM | PHOTO & TV SUPPORT TEAM |

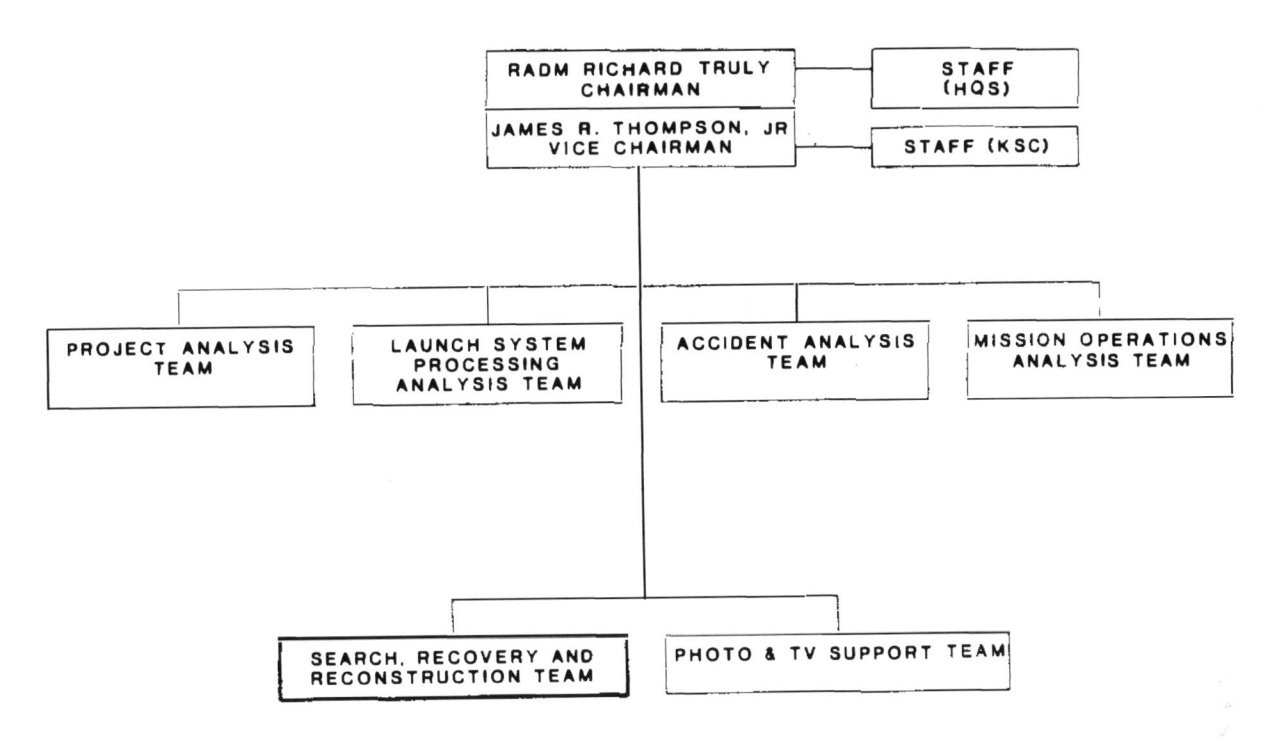

Exhibit 6. STS 51-L Design Analysis Force Organization

EDWARD A. O'CONNER - LEAD
COLONEL, USAF

E. H. WEBER - DEPUTY
NASA, KSC

WILLIAM SHEPHERD
NASA, ASTRONAUT OFFICE

MSFC TECHNICAL STAFF
A. A. McCOOL
W. L. RAY
KEITH COATES
FRED JANKOWSKI

PUBLICATION
W. M. MILIKIN, ROCKWELL, LSO
S. M. BUSTO, NASA, KSC
E. S. GRUHLER, NASA, KSC

SURFACE SEARCH AND RECOVERY
C. F. HENSCHEL
NASA, KSC

J. M. SHULTS
COLONEL, USAF-DDMS

UNDERWATER SEARCH AND SALVAGE
C. A. BARTHOLOMEW
CAPTAIN, USN

D. G. UHLER
NAVSEA

RECONSTRUCTION
S. E. KICKLIGHTER
NASA, KSC

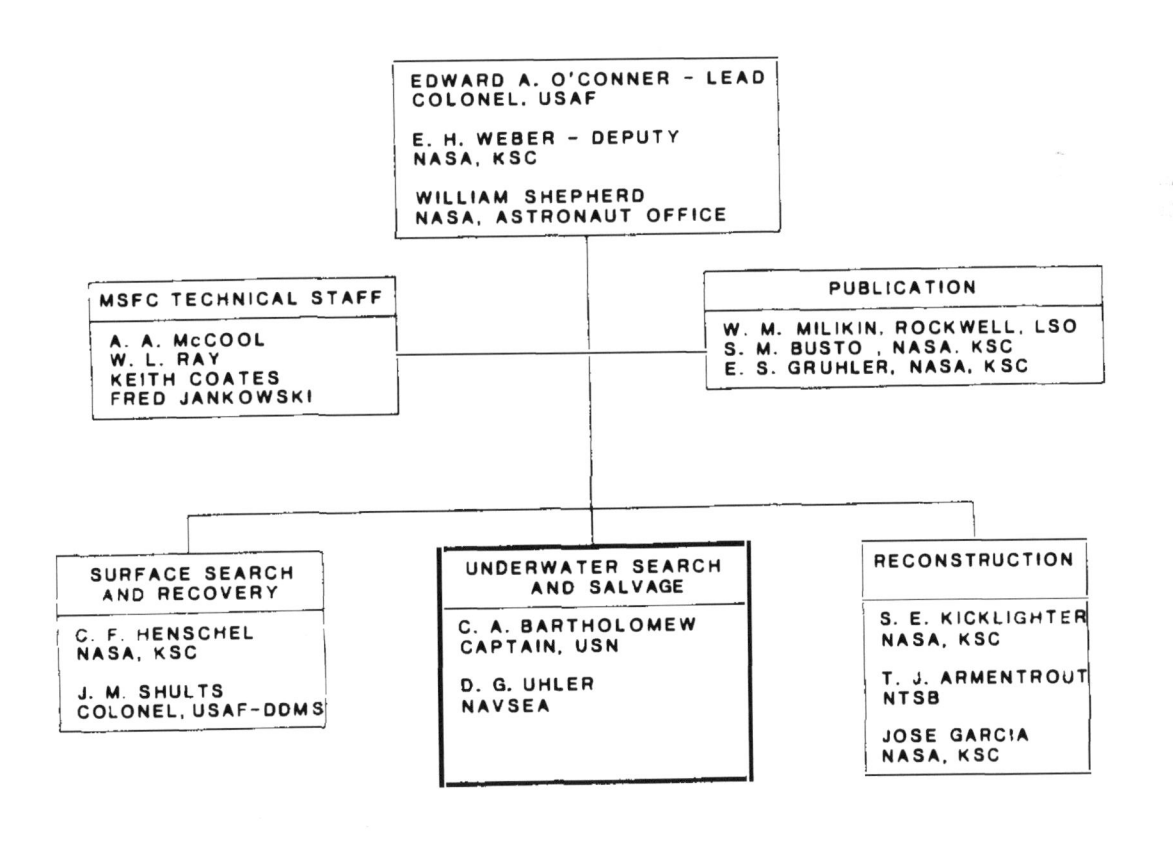

T. J. ARMENTROUT
NTSB

JOSE GARCIA
NASA, KSC

Exhibit 7. STS 51-L Search, Recovery and Reconstruction Team

2.5 Organization of Underwater Search and Salvage Operations. Organization and command relationships changed during the early phases of the operation which contributed to subsequent difficulties in the management and control of deployed vessels and search assets. There was a clear distinction between surface search operations (which continued until 7 February) and the underwater search and recovery which became a separate operation commencing 8 February. Some underwater search, however, occurred as early as three hours after the mishap. The NASA Marine Operations Manager (MOM) and the NASA LRD directed NASA ships in these early operations. During these initial search phases, NASA and USAF ships responded to the overall orders of the LRD for both surface and underwater search. As SUPSALV began to execute the methodical underwater search and recovery plan after 8 February, there was an increasing need for vessel traffic management. This need conflicted with both the operational control with which the NASA ships were familiar and the pressure NASA and its contractors felt to immediately locate and recover SRB and Orbiter objects. This effort, well intentioned but ill conceived, had led to ineffective, erratic and counterproductive results using inappropriate equipment and personnel. Resolution of the vessel traffic management problem incrementally improved after SUPSALV assumed operational control of all floating assets. The Navy organization for the underwater salvage operation is shown in Exhibit 8.

2.6 Supporting Forces. A number of military and other federal units and contractors supported the effort.

2.6.1 Ships. Several Navy ships were provided by CINCLANTFLT upon SUPSALV request (Appendix A, Exhibits A-3 and A-4). These units were USS PRESERVER (ARS 8), USS OPPORTUNE (ARS 41), USS SUNBIRD (ARS 15), submarine NR-1, and USS KITTIWAKE (ARS 13). Type Commanders COMNAVSURFLANT and COMSUBLANT dispatched liaison officers to provide operational and administrative support as required. The specific role of each ship is discussed later in this report.

2.6.2 Other Navy Units. Other participating Navy units included Service Squadron EIGHT, Submarine Squadrons TWO and EIGHT, Mobile Diving and Salvage Unit (MDSU) TWO, Explosive Ordnance Disposal Group TWO, USS GRAPPLE (ARS 53), Chief of Information (CHINFO) Field Office Atlanta, Naval Ordnance Test Unit (NOTU), Port Canaveral and several reserve MDSU detachments. SUPSALV was either on scene or represented by an officer throughout the operation. One or two staff civilian operations specialists typically were stationed onboard the ships or at the command post. The offices at NAVSEA served as home base for rotating on-scene SUPSALV personnel and supporting the operation with communications, contracting, financial and administrative functions. Several naval shipyards dispatched diving and salvage qualified engineering duty officers for training purposes.

2.6.3 U. S. Coast Guard. The U.S. Coast Guard provided assistance by exercising its federal authority to restrict unnecessary vessels from the search area and by providing strike team divers and occasional logistic support.

2.6.4 Naval Eastern Oceanographic Center, Norfolk, Virginia. ESMC provided oceanography and meteorology services and assisted the search analysis and plotting effort with telemetry data from radar and from visual records.

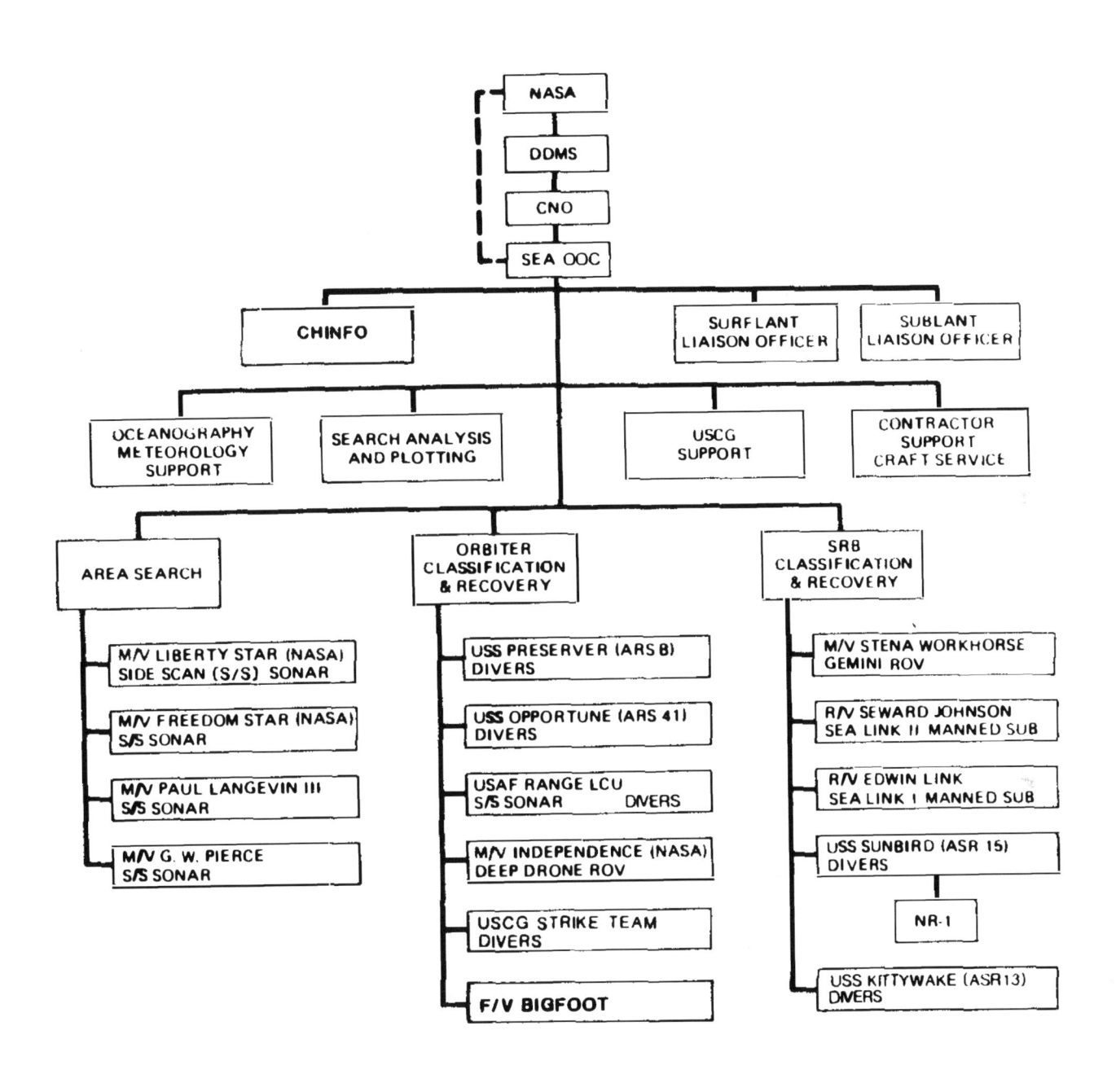

Exhibit 8. Navy Organization for Underwater Salvage Operation

2.6.5   **Contractors.** SUPSALV's ability to deploy a team of experienced contractors played a significant role in the recovery operation's success. Using these contractors as an integral part of the effort was essential because of individual expertise and contractor ability to provide highly specialized hardware, either directly or by subcontract. Each of the contractors was under a multiyear delivery order contract to provide specified services and equipment to NAVSEA. Therefore each contractor was required to perform within the scope of its respective delivery order without direct supervision by SUPSALV personnel. SUPSALV exercised control of the contractor effort by working with contractor project managers and by direct communication with floating assets using UHF/VHF or satellite communications systems. The principal contractors for the operation were:

Steadfast Oceaneering, Inc., Falls Church, VA. Steadfast Oceaneering, Inc. was SUPSALV's prime contractor for area search. Steadfast technical personnel analyzed NASA radar data and helped determine the initial and subsequent search areas. The company's search teams operated side scan sonars and navigation systems. The teams analyzed resulting sonar traces and participated in prioritizing targets for investigation. Steadfast personnel mobilized a computerized data management system for processing contact data and generated daily summary sheets and search charts.

Eastport International, Inc., Upper Marlboro, MD. Eastport International, Inc. was the prime contractor to provide SUPSALV with ROV and manned submersible operating services. Eastport personnel operated DEEP DRONE and GEMINI, subcontracted for SEA-LINK I and SEA-LINK II manned submersibles from the Harbor Branch Foundation and provided other miscellaneous equipment. The company also chartered and operated the ASD 620 and SCORPI ROV systems in support of the diver recovery efforts. Eastport engineers developed the tools and techniques to recover SRB wreckage from the Gulf Stream. Eastport personnel also developed a computerized cataloging system to manage the hundreds of photographs and video tapes taken of shuttle wreckage in support of salvage planning and actual recovery. The company's personnel worked along with NASA engineers to develop the plans used to salvage key portions of the SRB's.

Tracor Marine, Port Everglades, FL. Tracor Marine was SUPSALV's Gulf Zone salvage contractor. Tracor chartered STENA WORKHORSE and five other vessels for the search and salvage effort and also provided shore-based maintenance and logistic support administrative functions. Tracor, as SUPSALV's Emergency Ship Salvage Material (ESSM) base operator, also mobilized required support equipment from the east and west coast ESSM bases.

Oceaneering International, Inc., Houston, TX. Oceaneering International was SUPSALV's diving services contractor. Because STENA WORKHORSE had an operational 1,500 fsw saturation diving system installed onboard, Oceaneering was requested to inspect it and prepare it for use if required. Thus SUPSALV would have the option throughout the deep phase of the salvage operation to deploy saturation divers if requirements on the sea floor could not be satisfied by ROV's or submersibles. This diving option was never exercised.

Morton Thiokol, Inc., Chicago, IL. Under contract to NASA, Morton Thiokol, Inc. crews manned the three NASA ships, FREEDOM STAR, LIBERTY STAR, and INDEPENDENCE.

Chapter 3
PLANNING, LOGISTICS AND MANAGEMENT

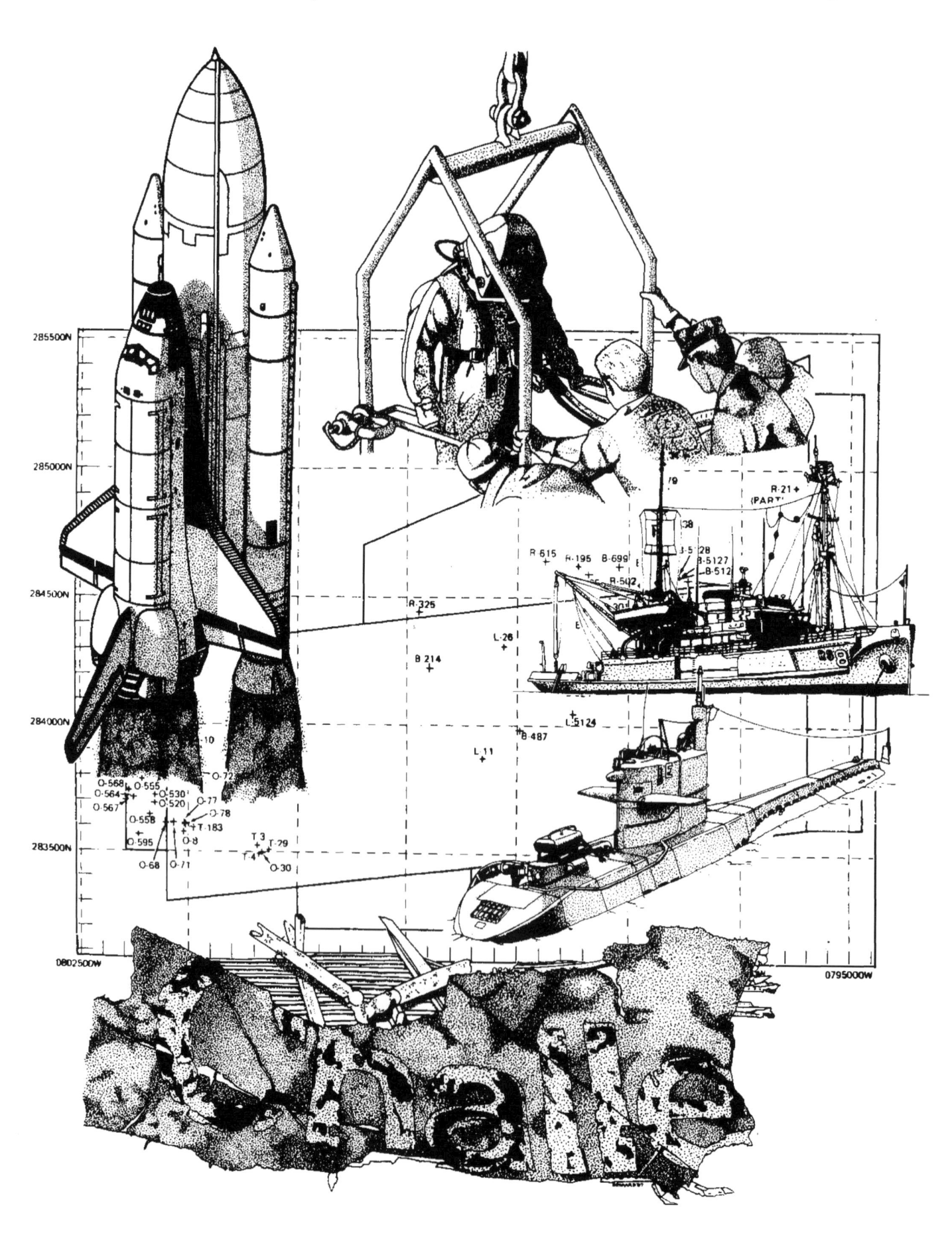

Exhibit 9. Navy Shore Command Complex

Chapter 3
PLANNING, LOGISTICS AND MANAGEMENT

3.1 STS 51-L Operations Plan. Planning was dependent upon a changing set of contact information, priorities and environmental conditions. The operations plan contained three major overlapping phases: search, contact classification and recovery. The three phases were to be accomplished concurrently due to the scope of the operation and the requirement for expedient recovery of key portions of STS 51-L hardware. The concept of operations was simple and straightforward and proved to be flexible.

3.2 Search. The search area, regardless of ultimate size and shape, would be searched using proven sidescan sonar techniques. The Navy procedure was to perform a methodical, comprehensive search of the entire designated area to maximize productivity of assets and probability of success and minimize long-term cost. Sonar contacts would be centrally evaluated and designated. Search platforms would not deviate from their track lines to either localize promising contacts or leapfrog to potentially interesting spots.

3.2.1 Ship Movements. All ship movements would be centrally controlled by SUPSALV from a shore command van complex, Exhibit 9.

3.2.2 Prioritization. Classification and salvage assets would be dispatched to specific targets based upon priorities which NASA and SUPSALV would establish.

3.2.3 Current. Because of strong northerly setting currents in the eastern part of the search area, ships would, of necessity, often conduct search lines in a southerly direction only. Although this would require additional repositioning time for conducting subsequent passes, it was necessary to obtain stability of the towed sonar "fish" while ensuring consistent fish speed over the bottom at two to four knots.

3.2.4 Contact Database. Assigned shoreside contract personnel would keep track of all designated sonar contacts within the search area, maintaining the database on a computer system located within the Navy command post. Contact information would include:

- Number designator
- Description
- Date found
- Location
- Size and/or number of contact items
- Orientation of the debris field (if applicable)
- Water depth
- Correlation with other available data.

3.3 Object Classification. Contact classification operations involved the collection of supporting visual evidence or documentation to determine the identity of contacts located during sonar search operations. Documentary evidence included still photography, video photography, diver descriptions and the recovery of small pieces of debris. NASA and Navy personnel reviewed and evaluated the supporting classification documentation and data to positively classify contacts. Three classification categories were used: STS 51-L Items, Non-STS 51-L Items, and Unconfirmed Items.

3.4 Contact Subclassification. Within the database, contacts classified as STS 51-L debris were further assigned to one of five major system categories: Orbiter (including payload), Left SRB, Right SRB, External Tank or Shuttle (if the debris could not be positively linked to one of the other categories). Contacts which were determined to be of sufficient weight to require attachment of external lift lines for salvage or to require special care in handling were assigned "major" status.

3.5 Object Recovery Priority. As a part of the concept of operations, SUPSALV assigned salvage assets in accordance with NASA priorities. Individual salvage plans for recovery of certain major objects would be prepared to provide for their preservation and protection from handling damage as well as to minimize dangers from potentially hazardous materials. ROV's would assist in deep water recovery operations while divers would work in shallow (to 190 fsw) water. NASA determined the following initial priorities for underwater salvage operations:

1. Right SRB
2. Orbiter crew compartment
3. Payload
4. Tracking and Data Relay Satellite System (TDRSS)
5. Internal Upper Stage (IUS)
6. Left SRB
7. Specified Orbiter components
8. External Tank (ET).

3.6 Logistics. Two factors contributed to streamlining asset assignment and mobilization and to effectively support the overall logistical effort. First, rapid mobilization worldwide is a standing procedure for SUPSALV and its prime contractors. Within a few hours after any tasking, each must mobilize anywhere in the world. Second, the experience SUPSALV obtains with the selection of a prime contractor requires knowledge of a wide range of equipment and its transportation and maintenance requirements. During the course of the operation, assets were be flown, trucked or shipped from every corner of the country.

3.7 Shorebased Support. Few major salvage operations have been successful in the absence of shorebased effort providing communications and logistic support of the work at sea. This situation was true with the CHALLENGER operation. To the extent that there was a smooth flow of communications between offshore and shoreside personnel, problems could be discussed and solutions developed. This communication was particularly helpful in planning lead times needed to obtain special equipment.

3.8 Mobilization. Mobilizing U.S. Navy vessels required authorization from their operational commanders. Commercial vessels were chartered by either NASA or NAVSEA contractors or were owned by the contractors. Tracor Marine coordinated operationally-related cargo shipments to and from Cape Canaveral. A NASA warehouse with access to the piers was the primary shipping and storage area.

3.9 Navy Shorebased Command Post. The Navy command post was an office van complex installed in the parking lot of the Range Control Center (RCC) building at Cape Canaveral AFS. It provided offices for SUPSALV staff and technical, logistic and administrative personnel. It was the center for sonar data evaluation and maintenance of video and sonar data recorders. The office facilities consisted of three portable offices. A forty-foot command trailer and a twenty-foot office van were shipped from the NAVSEA ESSM warehouse in Williamsburg, Virginia. A sixty-foot office trailer was rented locally. The command van complex contained the following equipment:

- One HP-9000 Model 520 computer
- Two HP-7580A high speed plotters
- UHF/VHF radio and telephone to satellite communications-capable ships
- Landline telephones (4 lines)
- Video system for reviewing and copying videotapes
- Office equipment, microcomputers, reprographic machines.

Exhibit 10. MAJOR DEPLOYED ASSETS

SEARCH VESSELS	LOGISTIC VESSELS	SUPPORT VESSELS/ASSETS
LIBERTY STAR	PELICAN PRINCESS	INDEPENDENCE/DEEP DRONE
FREEDOM STAR	ELIMINATOR	SEWARD JOHNSON/JSL-II
PAUL LANGEVIN III		EDWIN LINK/JSL-I
G.W. PIERCE II	**SUBMERSIBLES**	BIG FOOT/DRAG
LCU		
	JOHNSON SEA-LINK I	**SUBMARINE RESCUE SHIPS**
ROV'S	JOHNSON SEA-LINK II	
		SUNBIRD/NR-1 SUPPORT/DIVERS
DEEP DRONE	**SUBMARINES**	KITTIWAKE/DIVERS
GEMINI		
SCORPI	NUCLEAR RESEARCH 1	**SALVAGE SHIPS**
ASD 620		
		STENA WORKHORSE/GEMINI
		PRESERVER/DIVERS
		OPPORTUNE/DIVERS/SCORPI

NAVY COMMANDS PROVIDING TDY PERSONNEL

COMNAVSEASYSCOM
CINCLANTFLT
COMNAVSURFLANT
COMEODGRU TWO
COMSERVRON EIGHT
MOBILE DIVING & SALVAGE UNIT (MDSU) TWO
USS GRAPPLE (ARS 53)
COMSUBRON TWO
CHINFO
VARIOUS NAVAL RESERVE MDSU DETACHMENTS

3.10 Primary Assets. Exhibit 10 lists the major assets and commands participating in the operation. The overall effort required many types of search, recovery and supporting assets. No single vessel, vehicle or system was ideally suited for the diversity of conditions expected during the operation. Appendix B describes the vessels and equipment employed in detail.

3.10.1 Navy Platforms. Several U.S. Navy vessels were utilized based upon salvage and search capabilities and availability. Auxiliary Rescue and Salvage (ARS) ships offered necessary salvage and air diving capabilities. Auxiliary Submarine Rescue (ASR) ships could support air as well as mixed gas diving to 300 feet if required and could support submerged NR-1 operations. NR-1, a nuclear-powered Navy research submarine, was selected for its unique wide area search capability, extensive underwater endurance, video and photographic documentation systems and ability to travel below the strong surface currents and work on the ocean floor unhampered by the umbilical drag that limited some ROV operations.

3.10.2 NASA Platforms. Three booster recovery ships were immediately available on scene and used throughout the underwater salvage operation. These were the M/V FREEDOM STAR, M/V LIBERTY STAR and the M/V INDEPENDENCE. These ships were contractor operated for NASA and were intended primarily for ocean recovery of expended floating boosters and other support tasks in the coastal KSC range. M/V INDEPENDENCE was ultimately intended to support west coast space shuttle launches.

3.10.3 USAF LCU. An Air Force Range Salvage Vessel was also available and used extensively in shallow water recovery areas. This LCU (C115-1925) was used to support diving, shallow water search and recovery operations.

3.10.4 Commercial Platforms. Eight commercial vessels were chartered as follows:

STENA WORKHORSE. The principal deep water salvage vessel was STENA WORKHORSE. STENA WORKHORSE had dynamic positioning and four-point mooring capability, ample open space on the after deck for supporting ROV operations and 100-ton lifting capacity. The ship was constructed for offshore oil work in the North Sea and was an excellent platform for recovery operations considering the mandatory requirement for dynamic positioning in deep water, the expected weight of objects to be recovered and anticipated sea conditions off Cape Canaveral.

PAUL LANGEVIN III and G. W. PIERCE II. The research vessels PAUL LANGEVIN III and G.W. PIERCE II were used primarily for sonar search. Both vessels offered diving support capability, large clear deck areas and suitability for conducting underwater search operations. In addition, PAUL LANGEVIN III offered lifting capacity of 10 tons.

EDWIN LINK and SEWARD JOHNSON. The EDWIN LINK and SEWARD JOHNSON were chartered from the Harbor Branch Foundation to support two manned submersibles. Each ship also offered modest lift capacity, large clear decks and station-keeping ability. These ships had extensive experience working the Gulf stream at the required depths. Harbor Branch Foundation confirmed what SUPSALV had previously measured -- that water current generally diminished in a linear fashion with depth and was usually less than 0.5 kt on the bottom, which permitted unrestricted submersible operations. In fact, the slight bottom current aided the operation significantly by quickly dispersing the bottom sediments which were routinely disturbed by vehicle thrusters.

Logistic Support Vessels. The two logistic support and crew transfer boats, PELICAN PRINCESS and ELIMINATOR, shuttled among the at-sea ships daily, weather permitting.

F/V BIGFOOT. This boat, owned by Port Canaveral Seafood Company, was used to dredge the sea bottom in an attempt to uncover small pieces of debris.

3.10.5 Submersible Vehicles. SUPSALV historically has preferred remotely operated vehicles (ROV's) over manned submersibles for safety, endurance and lift capability reasons. Two factors complicated selection of ROV's for the operation. These were (1) depth of operations in the eastern portion of the search area and (2) the velocity of Gulf Stream currents. A number of ROV's were available which could exceed the 1,200 fsw depths required in the operation. However, because of the extreme drag against their umbilicals, few ROV's are capable of operating effectively in the current profiles experienced in and near the Gulf Stream. For these reasons two ROV's were initially selected.

DEEP DRONE and GEMINI. The Navy-owned DEEP DRONE was immediately available and selected for low current areas. The AMETEK-STRAZA GEMINI was chosen for deeper, high-current areas. Mother ships were NASA's INDEPENDENCE for DEEP DRONE from 8 February to 24 April and STENA WORKHORSE for GEMINI from 1 March to 29 April.

SCORPI and ASD-620. A third ROV, SCORPI, was deployed from OPPORTUNE (ARS 41) and began working 23 April to expedite classification of numerous shallow water contacts. A fourth ROV, ASD-620, was installed aboard INDEPENDENCE after 24 April and was used for shallow-water search and classification and worked in concert with divers between 1 May and 8 June.

JSL I and JSL II. The two manned submersibles, JSL I and JSL II, operated effectively in all water depths experienced during the salvage operation. They were capable of launching and retrieving in up to six- to eight-foot wave heights and each provided six to eight hours of bottom time per day.

3.11 Management. SUPSALV used the technical services of the many elements under its operational control to direct the operation and to interact with outside people and organizations. Once the authority of command was established for the operation and the assets were mobilized, operational success depended on managing the flow of information in order to direct people and equipment to the mission objectives.

3.11.1 Information Flow. Information flow was perhaps the most important responsibility of on-scene managers. Effective management of information ensured that all facets of the operation ran efficiently. The daily information flow is diagramed in Exhibit 11. Data from sonar traces, video photography, recovered objects or reports were carried ashore by PELICAN PRINCESS OR ELIMINATOR and delivered to the technical team at the Navy Command Post. Sonar traces were reviewed to locate all possible contacts. Data for all contacts were entered into the computer database. In addition, the database was updated to reflect information obtained from object classification and recovery. Each designated contact was tracked from initial designation, through classification, recovery and analysis as appropriate. A daily report and plot were generated from the database which listed current status of all contacts. The following records and reports were also maintained:

- Daily Situation Reports (SITREPS) from operational ships
- Master Event Log for STS 51-L Operations
- Sonar traces
- STS 51-L Salvage Operations Search and Contact Plot
- Sonar Contact Summary Evaluation Reports
- Search Line Log (cumulative)
- Field Notes on STS 51-L Salvage Operations
- Videotapes of Contacts
- Voice Radio Transmission Log.

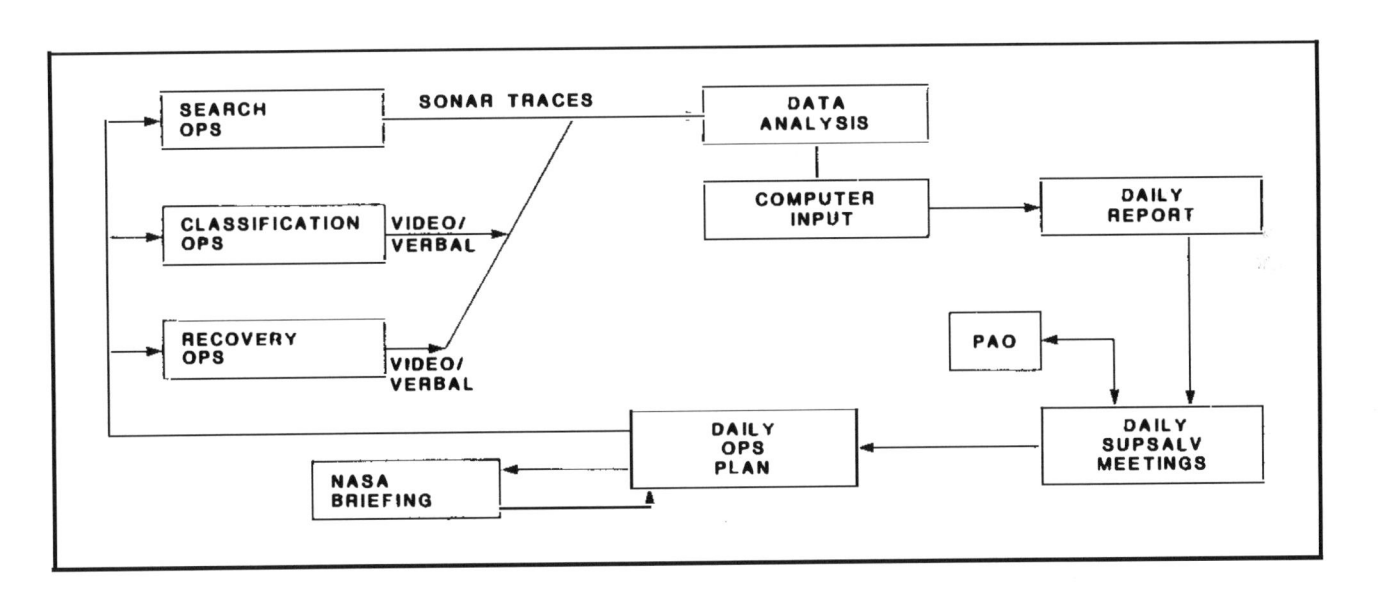

Exhibit 11. Daily Information Flow

3.11.2 Daily Plan. The UHF/VHF radios were manned 24 hours per day in the Navy command van by sailors from the USS GRAPPLE (ARS 53) precommissioning crew. SITREPS were transmitted to and from all at-sea vessels at 0600, 1200 and 1600 hours. At 0700 daily the senior SUPSALV representative met with his military and contractor staff to review the overnight data reports, logs and SITREPS in order to refine the daily plan for each of the deployed assets. Subsequently SUPSALV held a briefing for the Search Recovery and Reconstruction Team membership to verify priorities, finalize deployment of assets and discuss logistics requirements. All phases of the operation were discussed with alternatives planned if conditions changed. These meetings proved invaluable as they provided a forum to redirect assets, obtain new support and solve problems as information constantly changed.

3.12 Public Affairs. Public affairs was among the most sensitive activities in the CHALLENGER mission. LCDR Deborah Burnette, USN was assigned to the operation as the Navy Public Affairs (PA) Officer and she directed the Navy PA effort for two critical months. She normally attended the daily staff meetings at 0700 during which information was provided on the following:

- Location and planned day's activities of each search vessel
- New units being assigned to the search
- Debris uncovered
- Weather forecast and planned special operations.

Based upon information gleaned from this meeting, an approved press release was normally issued by 1100. PA responsibilities included fielding technical questions, managing the press, and responding to any emergency. To minimize the number of such PA emergencies, close cooperation between the NASA PA staff and the actual salvage operation via LCDR Burnette was important. SUPSALV and NASA maintained a constant PA information flow especially in new situations to allow the PA staff to inform and thereby manage the press. Some of the PA problems encountered during this salvage operation are summarized below (Reference 1).

- Lack of sufficient PA staff to deal with the large number of reporters who arrived soon after the mishap was a chronic problem that never was completely solved. At times press outnumbered PA personnel by more than one hundred to one.

- Disparity in background on the space program between veteran launch reporters and new arrivals after the mishap required a continual education effort. Background fact sheets were prepared and helped to alleviate this problem.

- Problems in NASA's public affairs organization impacted the Navy PA Officer in that for a time there was no clear chain of command for press information approval. The Navy PA Officer surmounted this by generating releases and submitting them via SUPSALV to NASA for approval.

- Enterprising measures were employed by the media to acquire additional photographs, monitor radio transmissions and break radio-telephone codes. Reporters used gyroscopic camera lenses for taking stable pictures from rolling boat decks and radio frequency scanners for intercepting transmissions. Therefore controlling access to sensitive information was difficult, requiring constant PA officer attention in issuing clarifications.

The bottom line, however, is that after the initial PA confusion subsided and an effective Navy PA organization was put in place, the U.S. Navy received excellent, worldwide media coverage. The work performed by U.S. Navy divers in particular helped to promote a very positive image to the nation of our diving and salvage community.

3.13 Financial Management. For the CHALLENGER salvage all financial matters were coordinated by DDMS. NASA funds were provided to SUPSALV via DDMS throughout the operation. Costs were tracked closely to stay within ceilings and to permit timely notification to DDMS as additional funds were needed. At the height of operations, daily NAVSEA expenses were typically $100,000 to $125,000 per day. The total USN portion of the salvage and search effort, including NAVSEA, contractor, USN ship, and transportation costs was approximately $13.1 million. Ironically, on 12 April while working with NR-1, SUNBIRD sailors retrieved a floating duffle bag which was found to contain a substantial quantity of high quality cocaine. After being turned over to the Coast Guard, its street value was reported to be about $13 million, just enough to pay for the entire US Navy effort!

Chapter 4
THE SEARCH

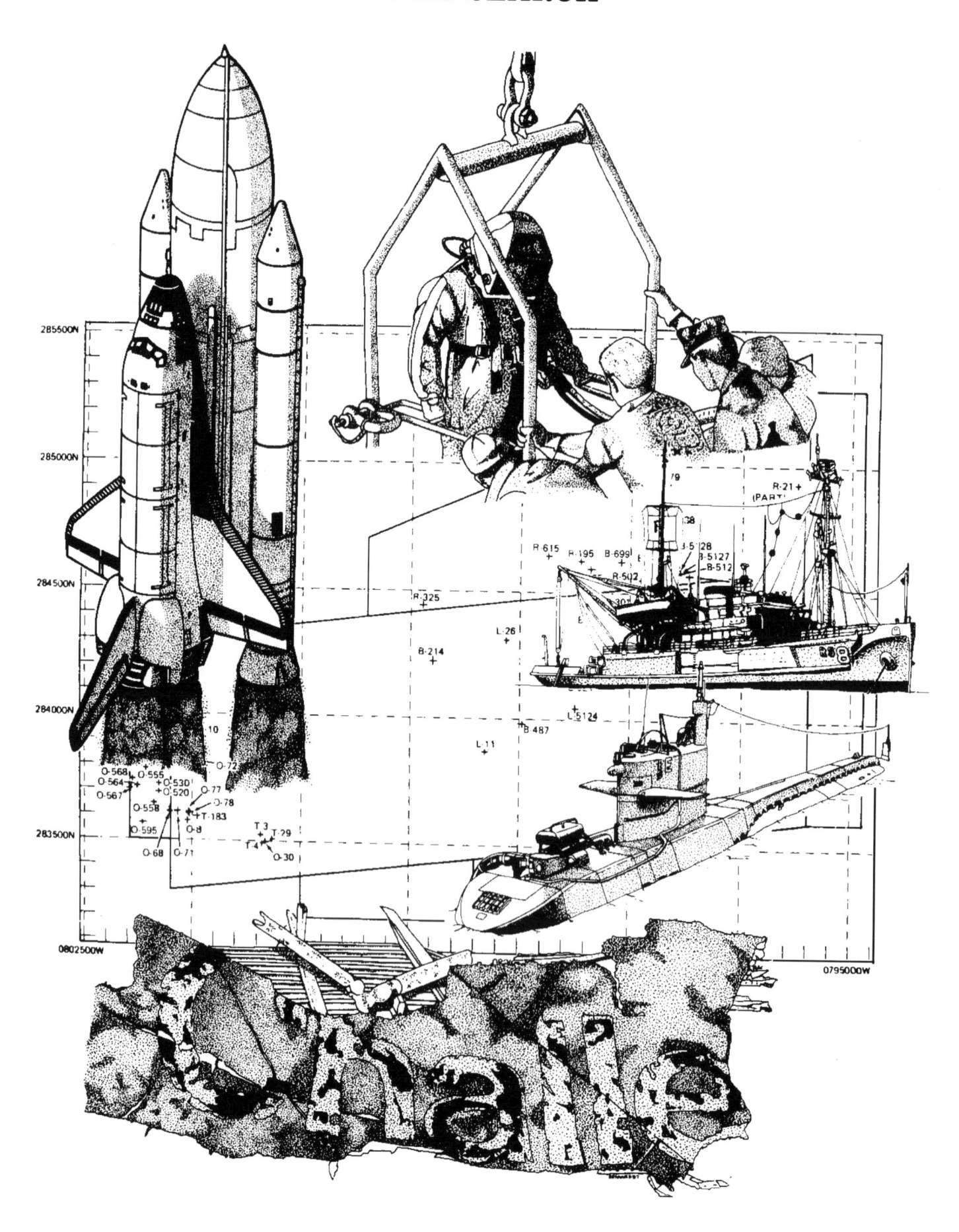

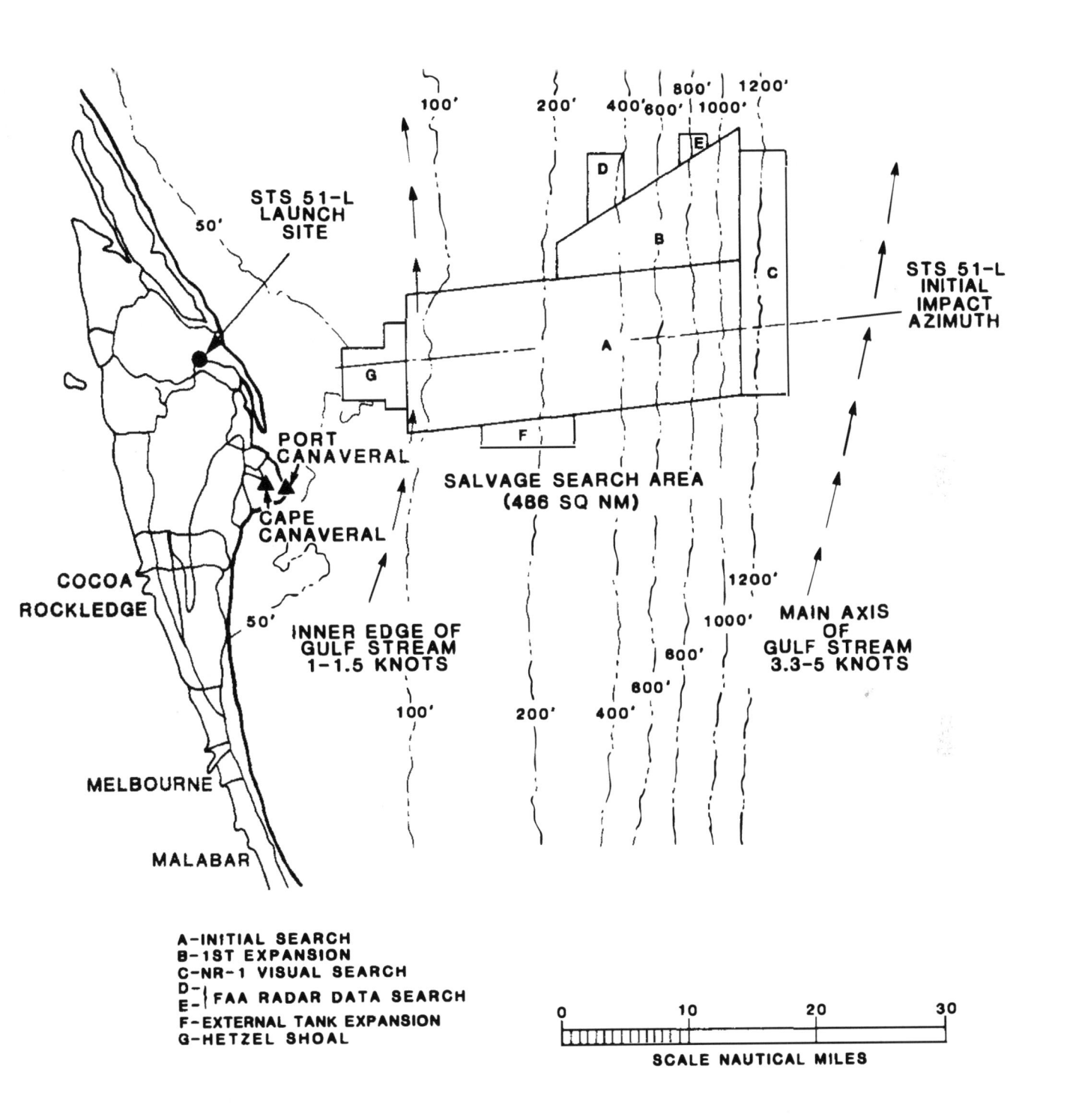

Exhibit 12. Final Search Area

Chapter 4
THE SEARCH

4.1 Search Area. The search area expanded and changed shape in response to additional telemetry data and the location of identified contacts during the course of the salvage operation. Exhibit 12 depicts the final search area totalling 486 sq nm.

4.1.1 Initial Search Area. The initial search area (Area A on Exhibit 12) established by SUPSALV was a parallelogram measuring 10 by 25 nautical miles. This area was chosen to be five nautical miles on each side of the azimuth along which initial radar tracking analysis showed to be the major STS 51-L debris impact points. The water depths in the search area ranged from 70 feet of seawater (fsw) to approximately 1,200 fsw. The initial search area was west of the main axis of the Gulf Stream but still well within its boundaries. Gulf Stream currents proved to be a significant impediment to the conduct of search operations.

4.1.2 Expanded Search Area. The initial search area was incrementally enlarged as the optical and radar data were refined and sonar contacts were designated and subsequently classified by divers, ROV's and manned submersibles. A right Solid Rocket Booster (SRB) debris field was found north of the initial search area and a debris field containing portions of the left SRB was located just inside the eastern edge of the initial search area. Further analysis of trajectory information and the location of these two SRB debris fields led to the first expansion (Area B on Exhibit 12). The search area at this point included approximately 370 sq nm. Area C on Exhibit 12 indicates the large area (3nm x 20nm) east of the initial area that was visually searched using the NR-1. The fact that no SRB debris was identified in this new area provided high confidence that the original search area's eastern border bounded most if not all of the SRB debris. As the search progressed, additional areas of STS 51-L debris and potential areas for debris were identified from FAA radar data and the search area was again expanded (areas D and E on Exhibit 12). Area F was added when external tank debris was located at the existing boundary. Finally, an area to the far west including Hetzel Shoal was searched from 2 May to 29 August (Area G on Exhibit 12). Exhibit 13 shows the overall distribution of the 881 designated contacts in this total search area.

4.1.3 Search Completion. The search formally commenced on 8 February using contractor search teams onboard FREEDOM STAR and LIBERTY STAR. PAUL LANGEVIN III and G.W. PIERCE (Exhibit 14), with search teams similarly embarked, were soon added and the primary search concluded 60 days later on 1 April. Search teams were then demobilized from G.W. PIERCE and FREEDOM STAR which were converted to classification and recovery. The remaining two ships provided sonar localizing support and searched a few additional areas including the Hetzel Shoal bulge until demobilized.

4.2 Contact Summary. From 8 February through 29 August 1986, a total of 881 contacts were designated from the sonar traces during the search, of which 711 were ultimately investigated using divers, ROV's, or manned submersibles. Of these 187 were confirmed to be shuttle-related, two were identified as aircraft, thirteen were shipwrecks, and another thirteen were determined to be debris from previous launches at the Cape. Some 112 contacts were miscellaneous scrap such as sinks, 55-gallon drums, old buoys, and rigging from cargo or fishing vessels. The remaining contacts were either geological in nature or nothing conclusive could be

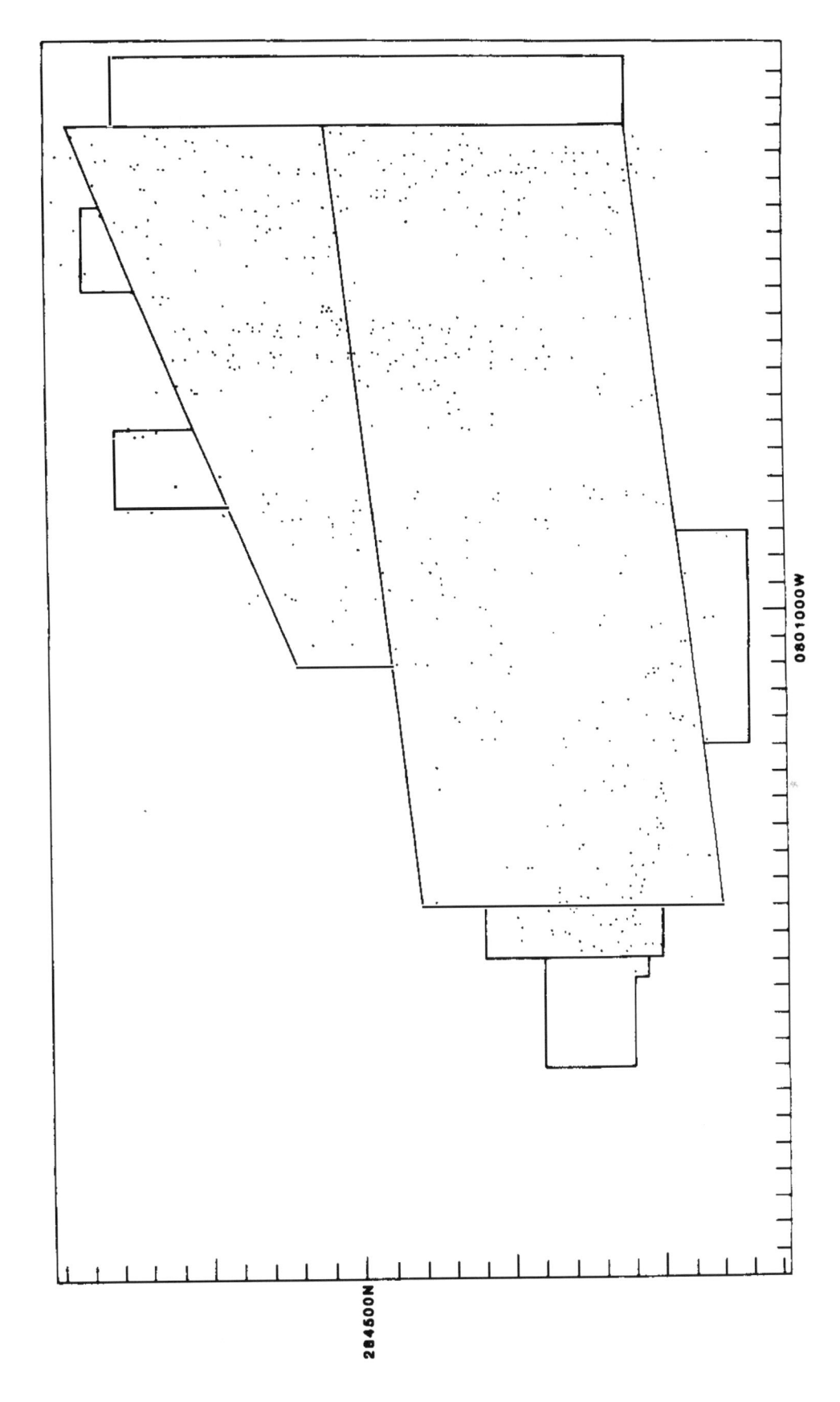

Exhibit 13. Distribution of 881 Designated Sonar Contacts

Exhibit 14. G.W. PIERCE

found. Care was exercised to accurately plot and keep track of all debris, as this information could be of benefit to future search efforts.

Right and left SRB debris fields were initially located on the eastern end of the search area. Orbiter and payload debris were located in the western end of the search area in relatively shallow water. Many of the individual contact locations defined debris fields which contained more than one, and in a few cases, up to 500 individual pieces of debris.

4.3 Selection of Assets - Search Operations

4.3.1 Search Platforms. NASA ships FREEDOM STAR and LIBERTY STAR were selected to support underwater search operations for the following reasons:

- On scene and familiar with local environmental conditions

- Good positioning and maneuvering ability and large, clear deck space

- Under NASA and ESMC contract and, therefore, immediately available with known costs.

Commercial vessels under SUPSALV contract were selected based on search and salvage capabilities as follows:

- M/V PAUL LANGEVIN III: immediate availability, diving support capability, large clear deck area, suitability for conducting underwater search operations, and lift capacity

- M/V G.W. PIERCE II: immediate availability, diving support capability, large clear deck area, and suitability for conducting underwater search operations.

4.3.2 NR-1. The U.S. Navy Research Submarine NR-1, LCDR Jim Holloway commanding, provided search and classification support to SUPSALV STS 51-L salvage operations during the periods 20 February to 18 March and again from 31 March to 12 April. NR-1 searched approximately 300 sq nm during 31 operational days. Operation water depths for NR-1 ranged from 150 to 1,312 fsw. During all STS 51-L operations conducted by NR-1, a NASA technical representative was onboard to assist with contact identification.

NR-1 conducted three distinct search missions during the period 20 February - 16 March: a detailed visual search at Contact #21 which at that time was hoped to contain the failed SRB section, an expanded sonar/visual search adjacent to Contact #21 and the aforementioned visual search to validate the eastern boundary of the search area. The collective outcome of these three search efforts was negative as they did not lead to identification of the failed SRB section. The results were nonetheless invaluable as they provided needed intelligence to more effectively continue.

Navigational drift of the NR-1 doppler system was expected to be 10 ft/hr in both the x and y axes. During the operation, drift was found to be up to 150 ft/hr for each axis and inconsistent. This navigational variation was later verified by location marking of NR-1 from the USS SUNBIRD, CDR Barry Holland commanding, which was then equipped with multiuser navigation equipment.

4.3.3 Navigation Systems

GPS/LORAN-C. The Global Positioning System (GPS)/Long Range Navigation, Version C (LORAN-C) integrated navigation system was the primary navigation system used by surface vessels. This system consisted of a Magnavox GPS satellite positioning receiver, a Simrad LORAN-C receiver and a Hewlett Packard computer/plotter system. The GPS/LORAN-C integrated multiuser navigation system receives signals from the constellation of GPS satellites and measures the elapsed time between the transmission and reception of the signals. In order to solve for the four position variables, x, y, z (altitude) and time, four simultaneous equations must be solved, which requires that four satellites be received at the same time with the assistance of an external reference oscillator (clock). However, the system can operate in times when only two satellites are visible. The accuracy for the unit in the dynamic mode is typically ± 15 meters.

At the time of the search, the entire planned constellation of 18 satellites plus 3 spares had not been put into their orbital positions; therefore 24-hour coverage was not available. Four-satellite availability was limited to approximately 6-8 hours per day, with two satellites visible between 12 and 14 hours per day.

The Simrad/Taiyo Model TL-888 LORAN-C unit was used for positioning the vessel when the GPS constellation was not available. The unit monitored all available time differences (TD's) in the selected LORAN chain, and computed the position from the best available TD pair based on angle of intersect and signal-to-noise ratio. During available GPS times, the Hewlett Packard computer kept track of differences between the LORAN-C and the GPS, and applied the resultant corrections to the LORAN during GPS down times. This ensured consistency among the various vessels involved in the effort.

LORAC-A. The U.S. Air Force Long Range Accuracy, Version A (LORAC-A) is a local radio navigation system operated by the Eastern Space and Missile Center (ESMC). The LORAC-A system was originally installed by the Air Force in 1961 to support Pershing missile launches and had been installed onboard the LCU.

Pingers. Pingers are small acoustic transmitters (37.5 kHz) which are used to mark objects for future location. The pinger transmits an underwater signal which is detectable by shipboard and underwater vehicle transducers. Pingers were used by ships and vehicles to relocate objects by tracking the signal azimuth to the source.

TRISPONDER. A Del Norte TRISPONDER precision line-of-sight navigation system was used to control positioning on the inshore portion of the search late in the task. The TRISPONDER is a line-of-sight system operating in the x-band frequency range (9,400 mHz). A master unit onboard a ship continuously interrogates two or more remote stations placed at known locations on shore. The GPS/LORAN-C and the Trisponder navigation systems both used the same HP computer/plotter systems with all equipment being provided by Steadfast Oceaneering.

4.3.4 Search Equipment. Side scanning sonar was operated from the search ships which tracked 300-meter swaths of the bottom. Sonars were provided by Steadfast Oceaneering as were several metal detectors used later in the operation.

Side Scan Search Sonar. Four Klein dual side scan sonar systems were used as the primary search tool for this task. The basic system consisted of an underwater towfish, a towcable and a graphic recorder. The standard side scan sonar towfish operated on a frequency of 100 kHz. A high resolution towfish was also used. Operating on a frequency of 500 kHz, the high resolution unit gave an extremely fine grain trace of bottom features and contacts. This allowed for a detailed analysis of the wreckage, both for preliminary evaluation of the contact and for picking out individual pieces such as engines, etc., from a typical debris field. The USAF LCU crew used similar side scan sonar equipment manufactured by EG&G.

INTAC. The INTAC system was used to assist in the job of calculating contact positions from the navigation data and sonar traces. Through sonar signal analysis INTAC calculated contact position and gave an estimate of contact size. Use of this system substantially reduced the time required to derive a position for the contacts picked from the sonar records.

Scanning Sonars. UDI and Mesotech scanning sonars were used with varying success to assist diving search operations. These units were deployed from diving vessels to assist in diver location of contacts. The system allowed the diving support vessel to position itself close to the contact and vector the diver, thereby reducing limited diver bottom time for searching.

Metal Detectors. Metal detectors were used to locate and define buried debris. Location of individual targets was not feasible without some type of sensor location system and thus the metal detectors were used primarily to define the limits of a buried debris field. Both towed and diver-held pulse-induction metal detectors were used.

4.4 Sonar Search Techniques.

4.4.1 Line Pattern.
The sonar scale used in covering the search area was 150 meters per side. Lane spacing was 135 meters, giving an overlap of 122%. The entire area was covered only once, and the 122% overlap gave at least two looks at all potential contacts. This large overlap, greater than normally employed, was sufficient to guarantee complete coverage considering the cumulative navigational accuracies being experienced plus an allowance for reasonable conning inefficiencies. Currents from the Gulf Stream affected the search patterns in over half the area as previously mentioned. With current speed averaging three or four knots, the search vessels were only able to conduct search lines when proceeding into the current. Traveling with the current at a sufficient speed to maintain vessel control resulted in an over-the-ground speed of more than six knots. At this speed, smaller contacts would have been missed by the sonar. Each of the four search vessels was responsible for ensuring that its area was covered completely and each vessel kept its own track plots of all runs completed. In areas where more than one vessel was searching at the same time, the ships maintained communications to ensure that their areas overlapped.

4.4.2 Search Data Processing.
Search vessels delivered sonar traces and navigation data by messenger boat to SUPSALV daily. This effort provided a consistent and accurate contact evaluation, numbering, and data management method and maximized on station time for the search vessels. Sealed bags were used to keep all records from the various ships separate and dry. Each bag was opened separately and data was first logged in. Search tracks completed were then entered

into the computer to produce up to date charts showing area covered for the morning meetings. The traces were then analyzed, contacts designated, positions calculated, and data both logged by hand and inputted into the computer.

4.4.3 Contact Priority. Contacts were assigned a priority number based upon strength of the sonar return, size of the contact, and its location in the search area. For example a good contact seven miles away from the left SRB track would not be assigned as high a priority as an average contact one mile from the right SRB track. This system was instituted after a sufficient number of contact investigations and identifications had been performed to allow establishment of some semblance of a pattern to the debris from the various shuttle components. Once instituted, however, the scheme cut down substantially on the number of contacts classified as non-shuttle and the distance the investigating vessels travelled between contacts.

4.4.4 High Resolution Sonar. During the final stages of the search, a 500 kHz sonar system was used in several areas of interest to search for small pieces of the Orbiter and cargo. As the range scales reduced, the search lane spacing also reduced. When lane spacing was 40 meters and then 25 meters, the LORAN-C system could not provide the accuracy needed to maintain the grid. The TRISPONDER navigation system was, therefore, set up in mid-July at the Cape Canaveral Light House and at a tracking station at the north end of Kennedy Space Center. Mobile units were set up on PAUL LANGEVIN III for searching and on INDEPENDENCE for conducting contact investigations using divers and the ROV ASD-620.

4.5 Final Search Results. During the course of the seven-month CHALLENGER operation, approximately 426 sq nm of ocean seafloor was meticulously mapped by side scan sonar. An additional 60 sq nm was visually searched by NR-1. If the linear sonar tracks of the four search ships were placed end to end, they would extend nearly 10,000 nm. If the paper sonar mapping traces delivered to the command vans were placed end to end, they would yield a single roll nearly 35,000 feet long. Within this 426 sq nm area, 881 randomly dispersed sonar contacts were ultimately designated. Subsequent visual investigation of these contacts enabled the salvage team to successfully satisfy all of the operation's mission objectives.

Chapter 5
CLASSIFICATION AND RECOVERY OF SOLID ROCKET BOOSTERS

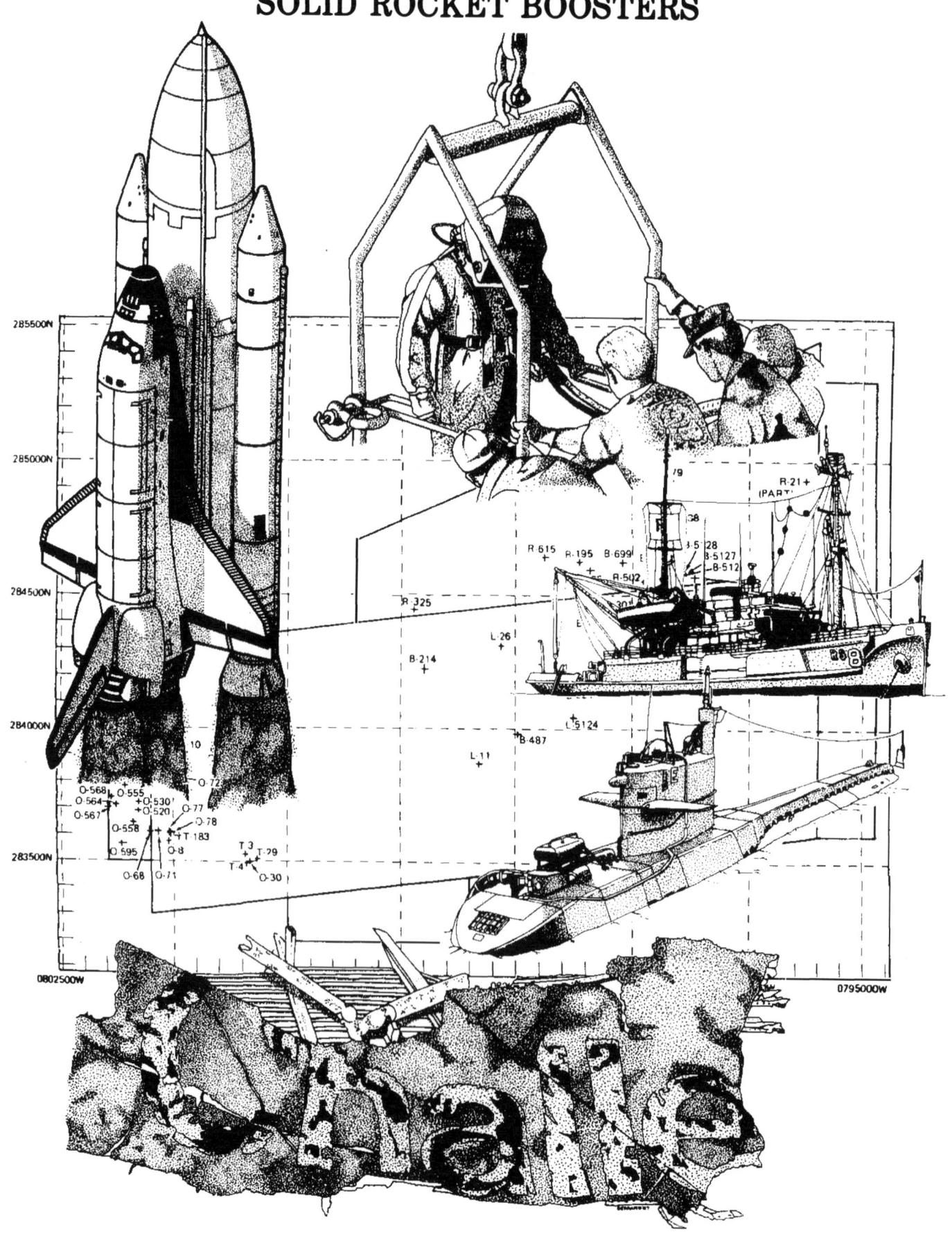

SPACE SHUTTLE
SOLID ROCKET BOOSTER GEOMETRY

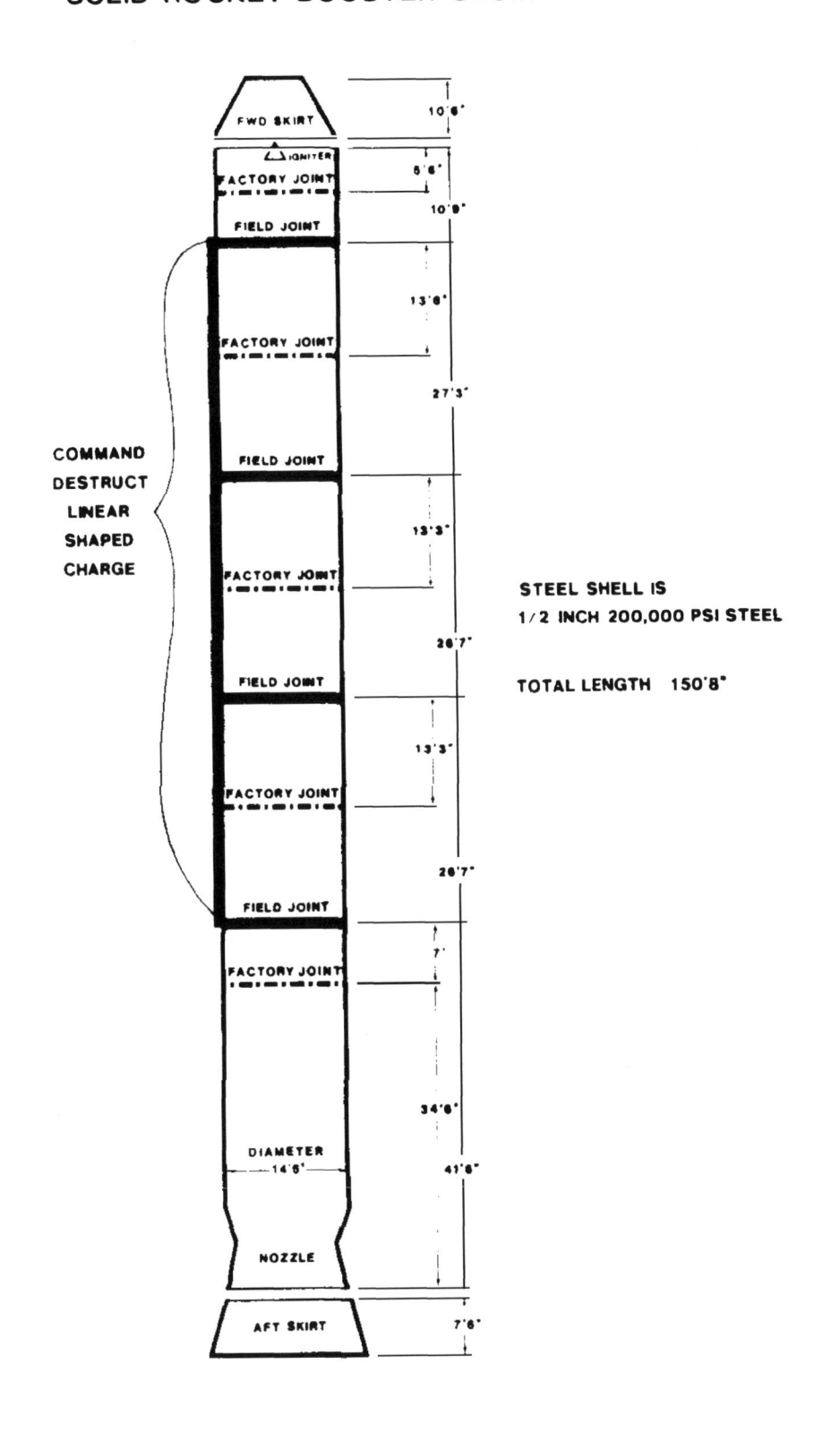

Exhibit 15. Arrangement of Typical SRB

Chapter 5
CLASSIFICATION AND RECOVERY OF SOLID ROCKET BOOSTERS

5.1 SRB Configuration. The primary mission of the deep water salvage operation was the recovery of the critical sections of the suspected burned-through joint of the right SRB. NASA had reviewed the shuttle design and photographic evidence from the launch and had concluded that the most probable cause of the CHALLENGER mission explosion was a failure of the right SRB lowermost field joint. At 0.678 seconds into the flight, photographic data and analysis showed a strong puff of grey smoke spurting from the vicinity of this joint at the 270 to 310-degree sector of the circumference. NASA believed that the lower field joint on the right SRB had failed, releasing burning gasses which ignited the liquid hydrogen-oxygen fuel in the External Tank and caused the catastrophic explosion. Exhibit 15 shows the arrangement of a typical SRB. Exhibit 16 shows the geometry and nomenclature of a typical SRB joint. NASA required physical evidence for proper evaluation of the failure. Another objective was recovery of other sections of the SRB for additional analysis. The salvage mission was successful in that the critical sections of the right SRB were retrieved and the majority of other SRB debris was recovered. Success did not come, however, without significant challenge from the environment and the SRB targets themselves.

5.2 Distribution of SRB Debris. Fragmentation of the SRB's at high altitude resulted in many small pieces being dispersed over a wide area. Exhibit 17 shows the overall dispersion of shuttle debris. The right and left SRB debris fields were co-mingled but were exclusive from the Orbiter, external tank and payload debris field. It must be emphasized, however, that this tremendous SRB debris dispersion was not initially known or even suspected. At first the debris fields found at Contacts #21 and #24 were suspected to contain the entire right and left SRB's respectively. Only after much later radar, visual and structural data analysis, supported by an emerging pattern from recovered debris of random SRB dispersion over vast areas, was the true nature of SRB disintegration correctly determined. In point of fact, when the range safety officer detonated the linear shaped charges, each of the nine joints (four field joints and five factory joints) on each SRB failed catastrophically. Six of the resulting ten "cylinders," already open at the 0° location due to the linear shaped charge cut, opened up and failed at 180° and in most cases again at approximately 90° and 270°, thus dispersing a "checkerboard" of steel plating from an altitude of 13 miles and at an initial relative rate of 100 to 250 miles per hour (mph) transversely and in excess of 2,000 mph axially. The two SRB sections aft of the rearmost factory joint, having the greatest mass, impacted the sea intact at the eastern most sites at Contacts #21 and #24. Structurally adjacent components of the right SRB were found separated by over seven miles. Exhibit 18 shows the distribution of SRB contacts along the failed field joint circumference.

5.3 SRB Classification. A comparative look at Exhibits 13 and 17 reveals the tremendous number of designated sonar contacts to be visually classified, a relatively small number of which would ultimately prove to be SRB related. Because of water depths and surface currents in the eastern half of the search area, surface supplied divers could not be used, and employment of DEEP DRONE was severely limited by surface current drag on the umbilical. Therefore, the task of SRB classification initially fell almost exclusively to the SEA-LINK I and SEA-LINK II submersibles. Occasionally GEMINI was utilized but that ROV's primary mission was recovery. Because of environmental, target dispersion, and vehicle endurance

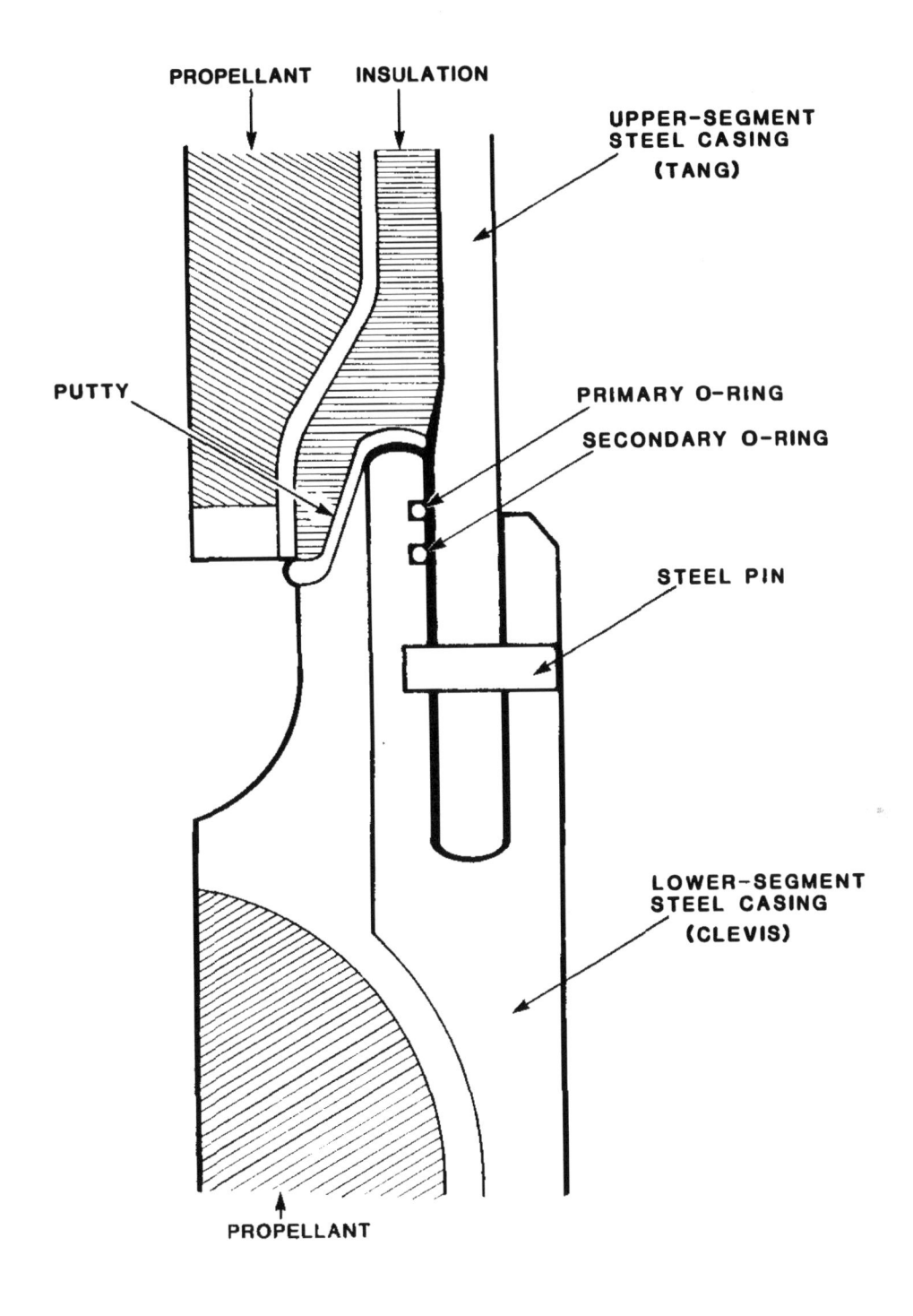

Exhibit 16. SRB Joint Configuration and Nomenclature

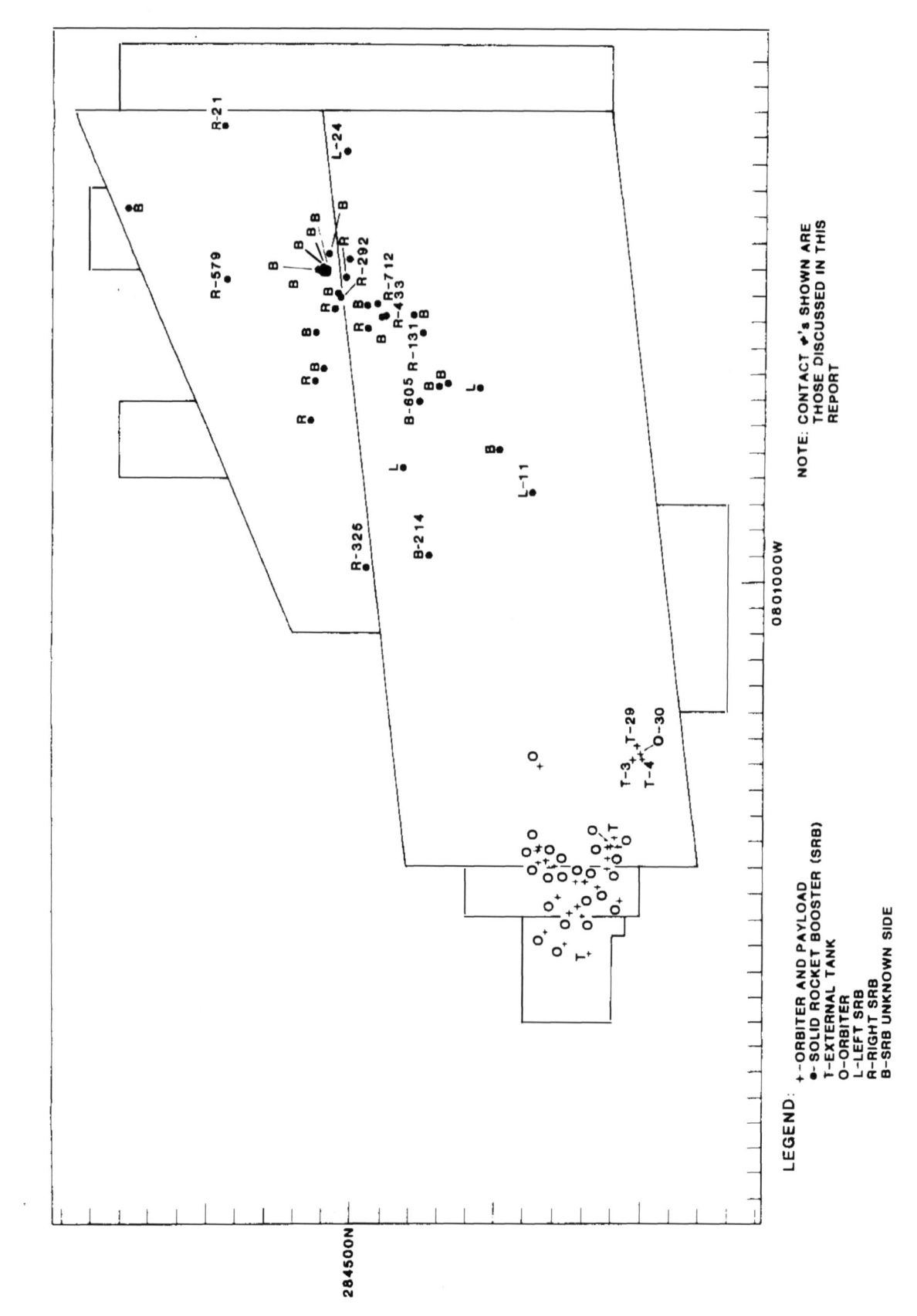

Exhibit 17. SRB and Orbiter Debris Areas

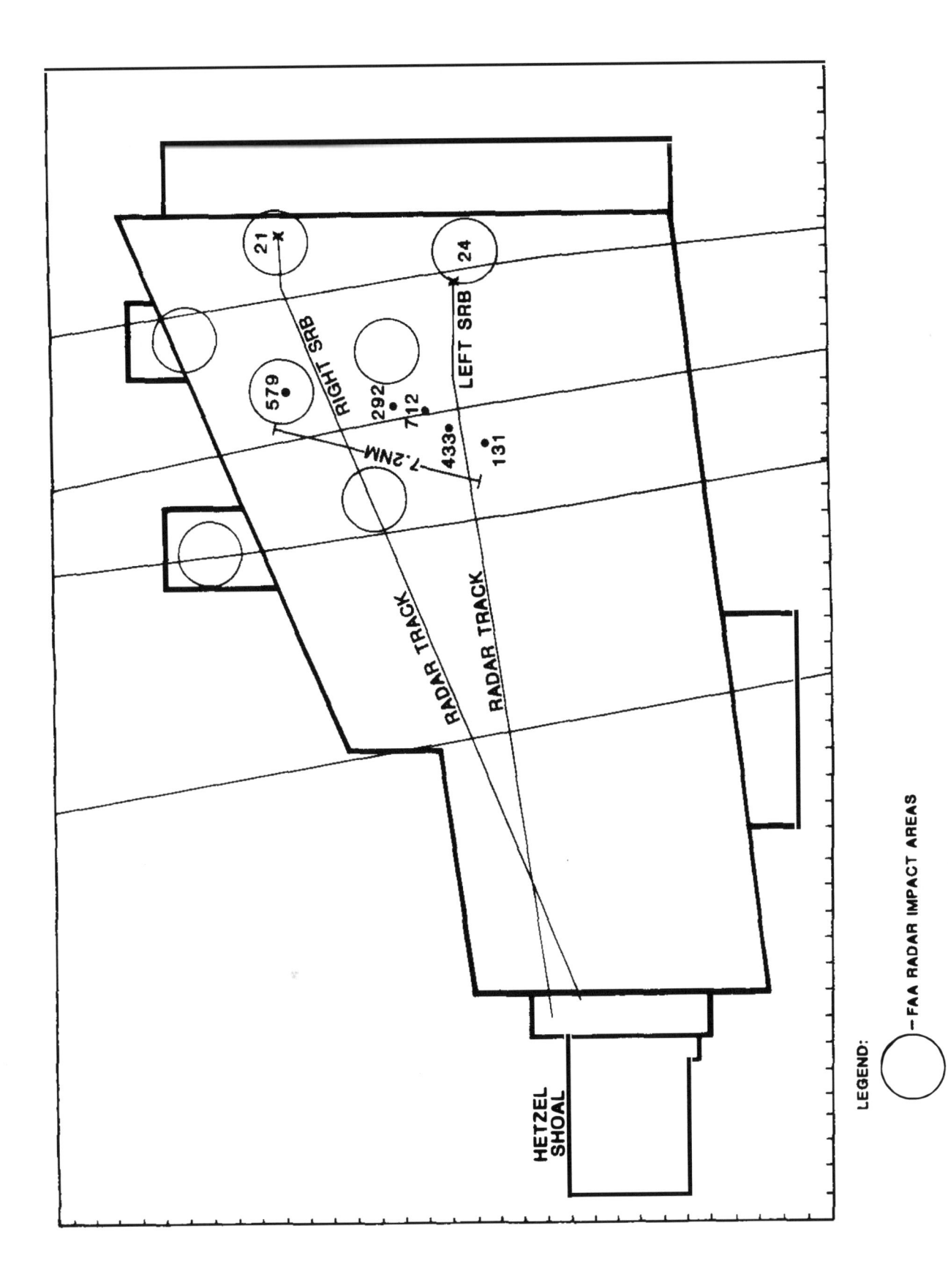

Exhibit 18. Distribution of SRB Contacts from Along the Failed Joint Circumference

Exhibit 19. NR-1 and Crew

considerations, the two SEA-LINK submersibles were realistically capable of classifying about five contacts per day.

5.3.1 NR-1 Classification Operations. In late March a backlog of over 300 sonar contacts had developed as the 60-day large area search neared completion. At this time SUPSALV elected to request the services of a mixed gas diving capable ship and NR-1 (Exhibit 19), which had been released from the search effort on 18 March (Appendix A, Exhibits A-5 and A-6 respectively). NR-1 returned on 31 March. This time, however, her support ship would be outfitted with the GPS/LORAN multiuser navigation equipment and NR-1 would be utilized exclusively for classification of already designated contacts. On 31 March NR-1 submerged and visually acquired Contact #605, a known SRB skin section. Navigation systems between NR-1, SUNBIRD and Contact #605's known position were initialized and NR-1 then proceeded to transit submerged from contact to contact. Periodically NR-1 would re-zero her doppler navigation coordinates by obtaining an update from SUNBIRD. NR-1 surfaced on 12 April. During that 13-day mission NR-1 visually classified 281 contacts essentially eliminating the backlog. Of those 281 contacts 22 were classified as STS 51-L debris including Contact #131, the section of the right SRB joint which was subsequently found to include the sought after burn hole.

5.4 Use of Recovery Assets. The assets described in Chapter 3 were deployed for SRB recovery as follows:

5.4.1 Heavy Lift Vessels. The primary vessels for heavy-lift recovery were INDEPENDENCE/DEEP DRONE with a 4.5-ton crane for the shallow and mid water areas and the STENA WORKHORSE/GEMINI (Exhibit 20) with a 100-ton crane for the deep water area. STENA WORKHORSE was specifically assigned this area because of the expected weight (60-80 tons) of the SRB components at the beginning of the operation and the high Gulf Stream currents. To cope with dynamic loading problems often experienced in deep ocean salvage operations STENA WORKHORSE was outfitted with a SUPSALV Fly Away Deep Ocean Salvage System (FADOSS). FADOSS consists of a large hydraulic ram for heave compensation and a 25-ton traction machine. Nearly all of the debris in the deep water (SRB) area was recovered by STENA WORKHORSE.

5.4.2 Remotely Operated Vehicles (ROV's). The primary purpose of ROV's in SRB recovery operations was to attach slings and lift lines for hoisting objects aboard the recovery vessels as previously stated. The GEMINI proved to be much more effective working in the greater depths and higher currents than DEEP DRONE.

5.4.3 Manned Submersibles. Manned submersibles were most effective in the classification of contacts in the deep water areas having high surface currents. NASA technicians aboard the submersibles were able to immediately verify contacts. As recovery procedures were refined, the submersibles routinely attached lifting pendants to the targets and dropped acoustic pingers to facilitate location and lift line attachment by GEMINI.

5.4.4 Attachment Tools. Because of the weight of most of the SRB pieces, the brittle manner in which the metal had sheared, and the hardness of the steel itself, attachment of pendants for a successful lift was oftentimes difficult. Although it had been anticipated that the rough edges of the wreckage would be quite sharp, salvors had had little experience working with the HY200 steel of which each SRB was constructed. HY200 is high yield steel with a tensile strength

Exhibit 20. STENA WORKHORSE Deploying GEMINI in Heavy Seas

of 200,000 PSI or 200 KSI. HY200 is nearly "tool steel," meaning that it could readily cut the relatively soft medium steel lift pendants. Versions of the following attachment tools were considered in SRB recovery work:

- Tang Attachment - Tang attachment tools were readily manufactured from commercial shackles. Because they were so easily attached by vehicle manipulators, they were the preferred and primary tool, as most of the SRB shell pieces had a tang section exposed. (Refer to Exhibit 16.)

- Clevis Attachment - Clevis attachment tools were manufactured but never successfully used. In addition to the specially designed tools being heavy and cumbersome, the clevis joints themselves had been typically damaged during breakup with the pinhole half being ripped away.

- Chokers - Lacking a tang section traditional wire chokers were cinched around the jagged steel sections. This technique was ultimately successful when employed, but many chokers were parted by the 200 KSI yield SRB shell steel.

- Plate Clamps - Specially modified plate clamps were used successfully where other techniques could not be employed. The clamps were designed to penetrate the rubber insulation and grip the underlying steel. This technique was used when no tang or clevis joint was available for attachment.

- Pyrotechnic Cutters - Pyrotechnic cutters with toggles had been developed for the 1982 STS-4 salvage and were available. However the likelihood of igniting unexpended booster propellant was sufficient to preclude use of any pyrotechnics.

5.5 Recovery Methods. Before the STENA WORKHORSE was dispatched to conduct deep water SRB salvage, the attachment procedures and lift techniques were validated in shallow water. Contact #11, a low interest, two-ton section of left SRB shell plate located in 215 fsw, was selected for this procedural validation. Both tang and clevis joint material was accessible. STENA WORKHORSE was positioned overhead. Attempts to connect attachment tools to the clevis joint were unsuccessful; however, a lifting pendant was easily shackled into a tang pinhole by GEMINI. On a second dive GEMINI snapped the main lift line to the pendant and the lift was successfully performed. STENA WORKHORSE was ready to go to work. Either GEMINI or one of the SEA-LINK submersibles could be used to attach lifting pendants. A typical SEA-LINK I attachment sequence follows:

- The SEWARD JOHNSON would position herself up current from the target site and SEA-LINK I was rigged with a shackle-type attachment tool with wire pendant. Alternatively, a wire choke or plate clamp was rigged in the manipulator for lifting pieces without accessible joint pin holes (tang end).

- The submersible was launched and dived to the sea floor, guided to the target by the sonar return.

- Once the target was visually located, the submersible maneuvered to optically inspect the debris.

- The manipulator was used to attach the shackle to an exposed joint pin hole. Alternately, a sling choker was cinched around the target or a plate clamp attached.

- With the attachment complete, the rigging was inspected and, if satisfactory, a pinger was deployed (optional) and SEA-LINK I would depart the site.

Bringing the lift line to the target site and connecting to the target with the ROV was made difficult by the high currents, often poor bottom visibility, and small, low targets providing poor sonar contact. During the first few lifts, the one-inch diameter kevlar lift line was reaved through a block on the STENA WORKHORSE's 100-ton boom tip, through a fairlead block on deck, the FADOSS ram and finally to the FADOSS winch. After several lifts were completed, it became apparent the SRB pieces were smaller than originally anticipated and that STENA WORKHORSE was stable enough to dispense with the FADOSS and reave the kevlar directly to the faster STENA WORKHORSE installed winch. This scheme was used for the remainder of the salvage operations. Exhibit 21 shows the configuration of the STENA WORKHORSE and GEMINI. A typical sequence of tasks follows:

- About 200 feet from the end of the line, a two-ton clump of anchor chain segments was attached with a stopper. This served to hold the lift line nearly vertical in the current.

- A kevlar line below the clump was loosely faked and fastened in place with plastic tie-ties near the clump. The bitter end of this whip was rigged so that it pulled away from the clump in short lengths rather than all at once. On the end of the whip was a snap hook with a handle for the ROV manipulator to facilitate attachment to the target's preattached lifting pendant.

- The ROV maneuvered to the target site pulling the whip behind, taking care when maneuvering to prevent entanglements.

- At the target site, the ROV relocated the lift sling and attached the recovery line. The ROV stayed on site until tension was placed on the lift line to verify that the rigging was sound.

- When the ROV was safely back onboard STENA WORKHORSE, the target was hauled up until the chain clump was alongside. The clump was then lifted on deck and cut loose from the lift line. The lift continued until the target piece was landed and secured to the deck. NASA and Explosive Ordnance Disposal personnel would immediately inspect the debris and prepare it for transit and storage.

The time required for target verification, recovery pendant attachment, and lift line rigging ranged from 2 to over 12 hours of actual vehicle bottom time.

5.6 Safety and Hazards

5.6.1 Ordnance.
Ordnance handling and disposal personnel were an integral part of SRB salvage. It was thought that the separation of the SRB from the External Tank occurred before engagement of the Pyro Initiator Circuit (PIC), which controls the various pyrotechnic devices on the SRB. Therefore, all ordnance devices on the SRB's were assumed live during the retrieval operations and handled with extreme care. The parts were stabilized prior to loading onto the decks of the ships and were lashed down immediately. Ordnance was disarmed by onboard EOD personnel as necessary. Hydrazine tanks located in the aft skirt were inspected for leakage prior to personnel approaching the SRB debris.

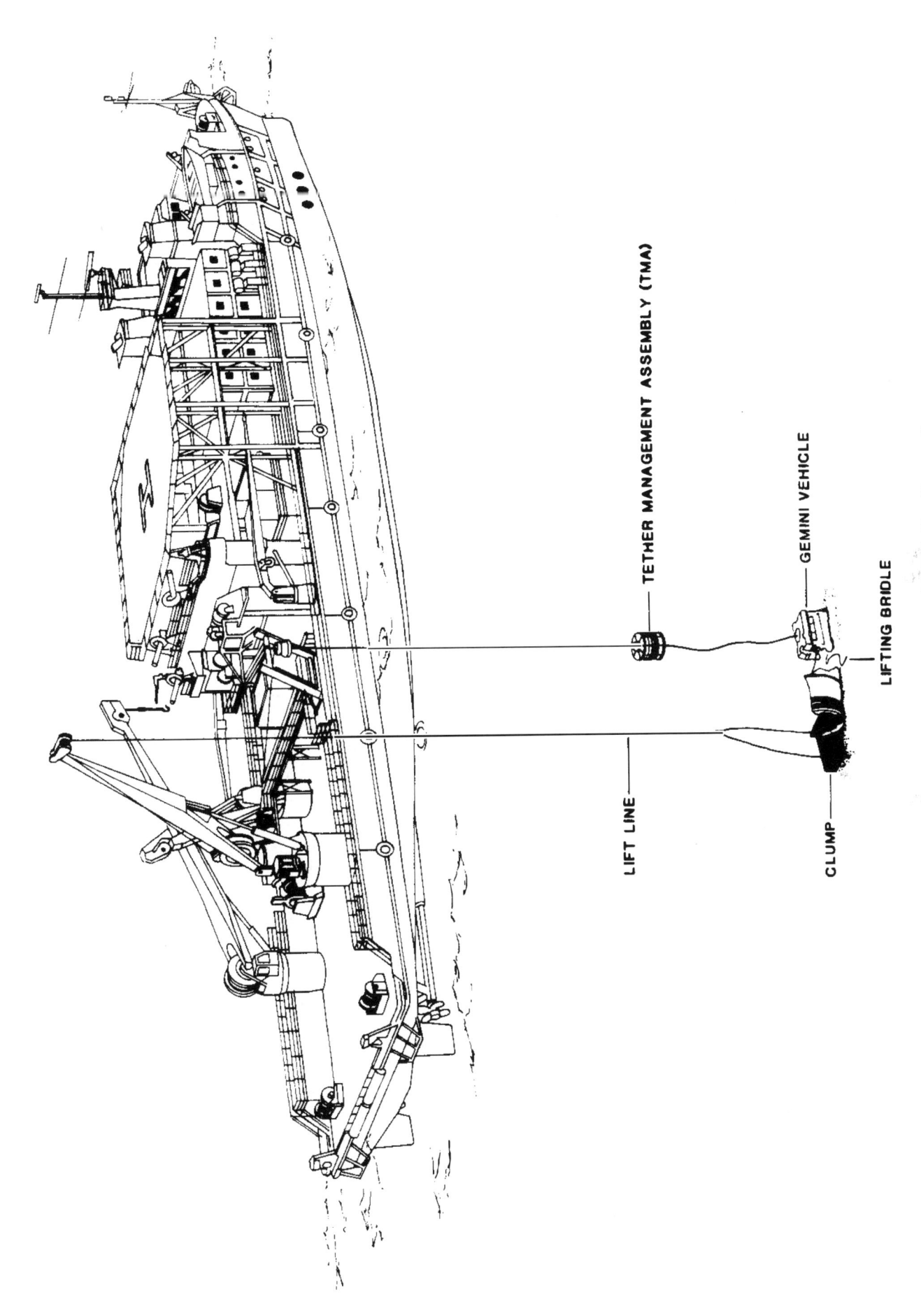

Exhibit 21. STENA WORKHORSE and GEMINI Configuration

5.6.2 Propellent. Unexpended solid rocket propellent was extremely hazardous and required precautions to prevent ignition. The SRB propellent burns at temperatures in excess of 5,000° F and tended to become unstable with emersed time. Recovered parts containing propellent were kept wet and care was taken to avoid shear or sparking between hard surfaces while handling. Open flames and direct heat were kept away. Once offloaded ashore SRB parts containing propellent were taken to an ordnance burn area where the propellent was safely ignited before the part was taken to the reconstruction area for analysis. Exhibit 22 shows the burning of propellent from a booster piece.

5.7 STENA WORKHORSE SRB Recovery. After the successful recovery procedure validation using Contact #11 on 7 March, STENA WORKHORSE was continuously employed salving SRB components until demobilization on 29 April. During this period 91 GEMINI dives were conducted and 38 major SRB targets salved. On 17 March the first shell piece on the suspect right SRB joint (Contact #292) was recovered. Based upon the NR-1 classification mission results, four additional pieces from this joint were recovered (Contacts #579, #131, #433-1 and #433-2). The final SRB target (Contact #712) was recovered on 28 April. Throughout the operation efforts were hampered by weather, current and GEMINI ROV maintenance/downtime problems. Each target presented its unique set of problems which were analyzed and overcome. After recovery, debris was delivered ashore and transported from the Naval Ordnance Test Unit (NOTU) berths through Cape Canaveral AFS to KSC for analysis and evaluation by NASA and National Transportation Safety Board (NTSB) personnel.

5.8 Submarine Rescue Ship SRB Recovery. Both USS SUNBIRD (when not escorting NR-1) and USS KITTIWAKE, LCDR T.J. Erwin commanding, were available to provide diving services during discrete periods. KITTIWAKE's services had originally been requested on 12 March to assist in the classification and possible recovery of approximately 50 sonar contacts backlogged in 150-300 fsw depths using mixed gas divers, (Appendix A, Exhibit A-5). When she finally arrived on 11 April, however, the NR-1 had already cleared the contact backlog and the requirement for mixed gas diving no longer existed. However the SUNBIRD and KITTIWAKE were each assigned one SRB shell target for recovery. On 14-15 April SUNBIRD entered a two point moor and recovered Contact #325 from 177 fsw using MK 1 lightweight air equipment. On 17 April KITTIWAKE entered a two point moor and recovered Contact #214 from 175 fsw using MK 12 SSDS air equipment. Both ships were also assigned to provide miscellaneous orbiter recovery diving services for brief periods.

5.9 Recovery of the Right SRB Critical Joint. The recovery of Contact #131 typifies the successful result of the concept of operations wherein several major assets were sequentially utilized to locate and recover the target. Contact #131 was the right SRB aft center segment containing the tang portion of the joint burn through area, Exhibit 23. This contact was initially located on 1 March 1986 by LIBERTY STAR in 560 feet of water using side scanning sonar. At that time the magnitude of SRB dispersion was not known and its location was in the left SRB trajectory area. Thus it was assigned a low priority for classification. NR-1 operated at the site of Contact #131 on 5 April, classified the contact as probable STS 51-L debris and videotaped the contact. After a review of the NR-1 videotape by SUPSALV and NASA engineers, visual evidence of possible burned areas raised its priority markedly and the manned submersible SEA-LINK I, operating from EDWIN LINK, was assigned to investigate the contact. On a dive conducted on 12 April 1986, SEA-LINK I onboard observers verified that Contact #131 was badly burned and scarred. A wire pendant was attached to a tang section and a pinger

Exhibit 22. Propellant Burning from a Booster Piece

deployed. STENA WORKHORSE was immediately assigned to conduct recovery. Using the ROV GEMINI, STENA WORKHORSE attached a lift line and recovered the piece on 13 April 1986, Exhibit 24.

The salvage of Contact #131 involved three surface vessels, a side scanning sonar, a research submarine, a manned submersible, an ROV and a deep ocean salvage ship. Similarly the recovery of the other significant contacts aft such as Contact #712 (Exhibit 25) and most of the other pieces of SRB shell required the use of multiple assets to successfully locate, classify and recover.

5.10 Completion of SRB Recovery Operations. With the recovery of Contact #131 the primary objective of the deep water SRB salvage operations had been satisfied. Nonetheless NASA requested that the lower or companion piece containing the other half of the burned through joint also be recovered for investigative purposes. However detailed visual classification and recovery efforts of all designated sonar contacts in the known SRB debris field confirmed that the companion piece had not yet been found. An initiative to research with side scan sonar the most probable area was abandoned by SUPSALV in favor of reanalyzing existing sonar traces. A 72 sq nm area bounded by lat 28° 50 min - 28° 42 min and long 79° 55 min - 80° 04 min was defined. By exercising greater discrimination, the sonar trace evaluation team designated 15 additional contacts within this box, two of which were subsequently found to be SRB related. Contact #712 had been located by side scan sonar on 11 March. However, because it was considered marginal, it had not been designated as a contact at that time. On 18 April it was designated along with 14 other contacts. STENA WORKHORSE positioned herself over Contact #712 on 26 April and the GEMINI ROV classified it as SRB. Tang holes were not accessible so a plate grabber was rigged. During recovery the plate grabber slipped off and the target fell to the bottom. In its new attitude, a tang section was exposed, a shackle attached, and the piece was successfully retrieved and landed on deck. This entire operation required four ROV dives over a 22-hour period. STENA WORKHORSE recovered two final SRB targets and proceeded into Port Canaveral the afternoon of 28 April to offload debris and commence demobilization. Exhibit 26 shows a composite of the major pieces recovered along the failed joint. Exhibit 27 shows a full size reconstruction of the booster shell from one inch styrofoam templates patterned from the recovered pieces. The two pieces, Contacts #131 and #712, as shown fitted together, reveal a 28-inch diameter circular burnhole, portions of which looked as if they had been cut by an oxy-acetylene torch. The exact cause of the space shuttle CHALLENGER explosion was confirmed.

5.11 SRB Recovery Summary. The following data summarize the extent of the effort involved in the SRB salvage:

Total weight of both SRB shells	196,726 pounds
Total weight recovered	102,500 pounds
Total weight found but not recovered	54,000 pounds
Total weight not found or "lost" in inventory	40,226 pounds
Total pieces recovered	42 pieces
Average weight per piece	2,440 pounds
Heaviest piece recovered	11,000 pounds
Percent located	80 %
Percent recovered	52 %
Deepest SRB piece recovered	1,295 feet
Shallowest SRB piece recovered	168 feet
Number of GEMINI ROV dives	102 dives

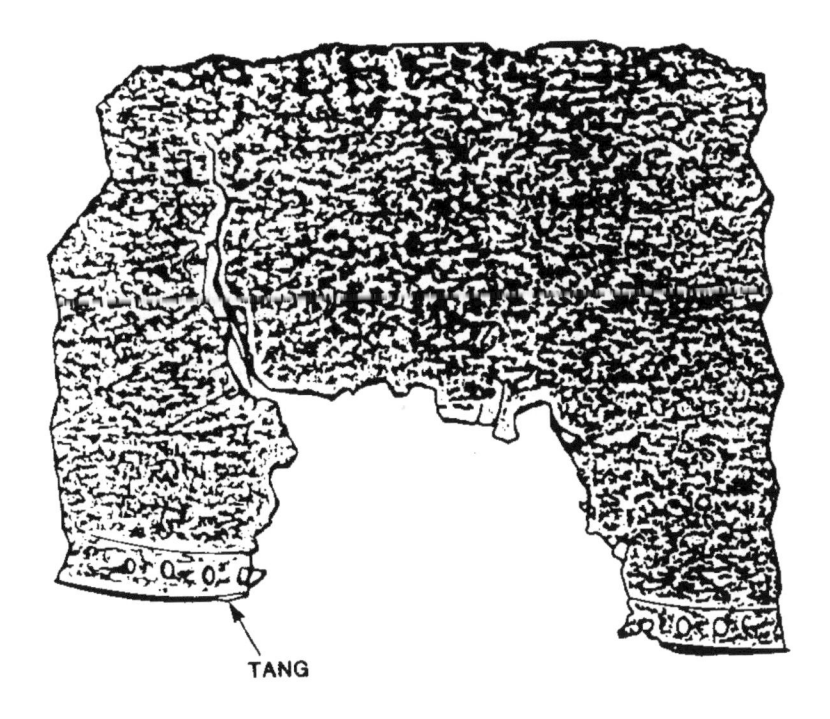

INTERIOR SURFACE

EXTERIOR SURFACE

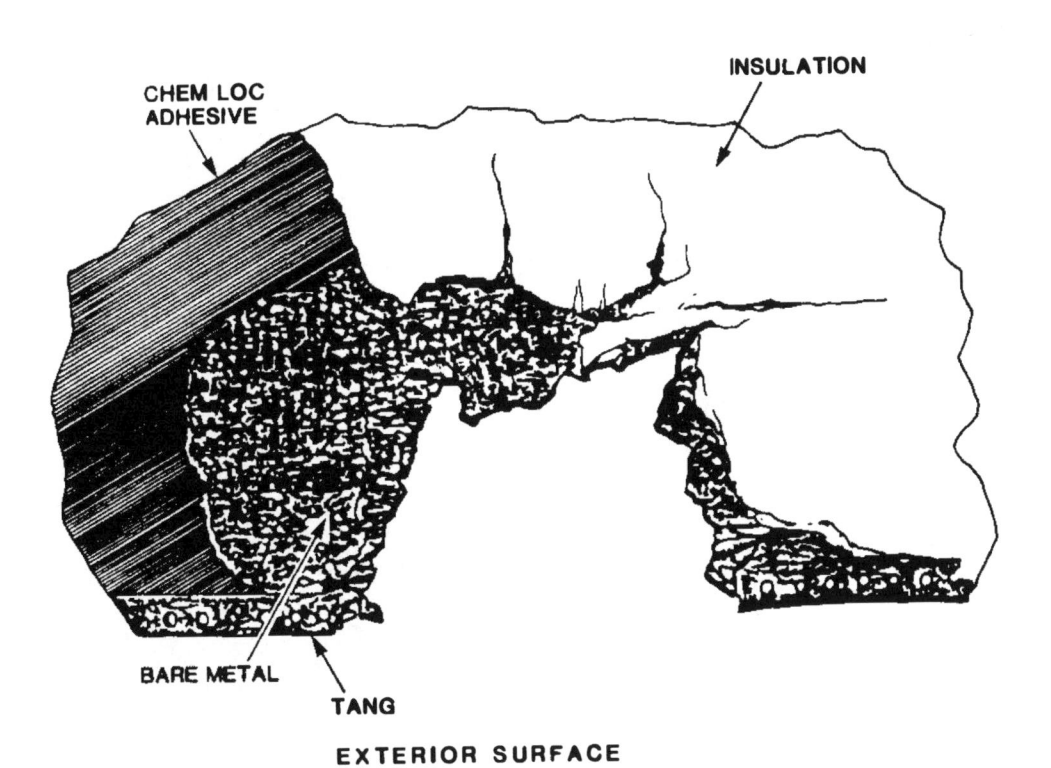

Exhibit 23. Contact #131 Interior and Exterior Surfaces

Exhibit 24. Contact #131 Recovery Right SRB

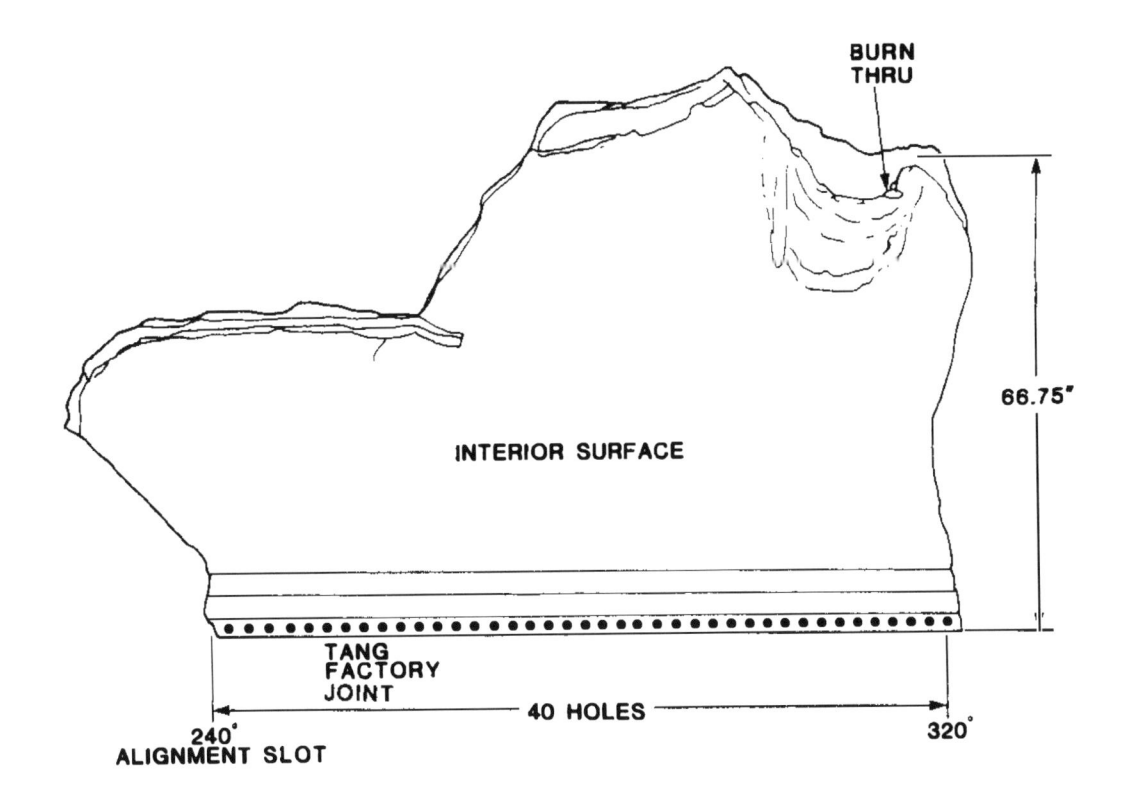

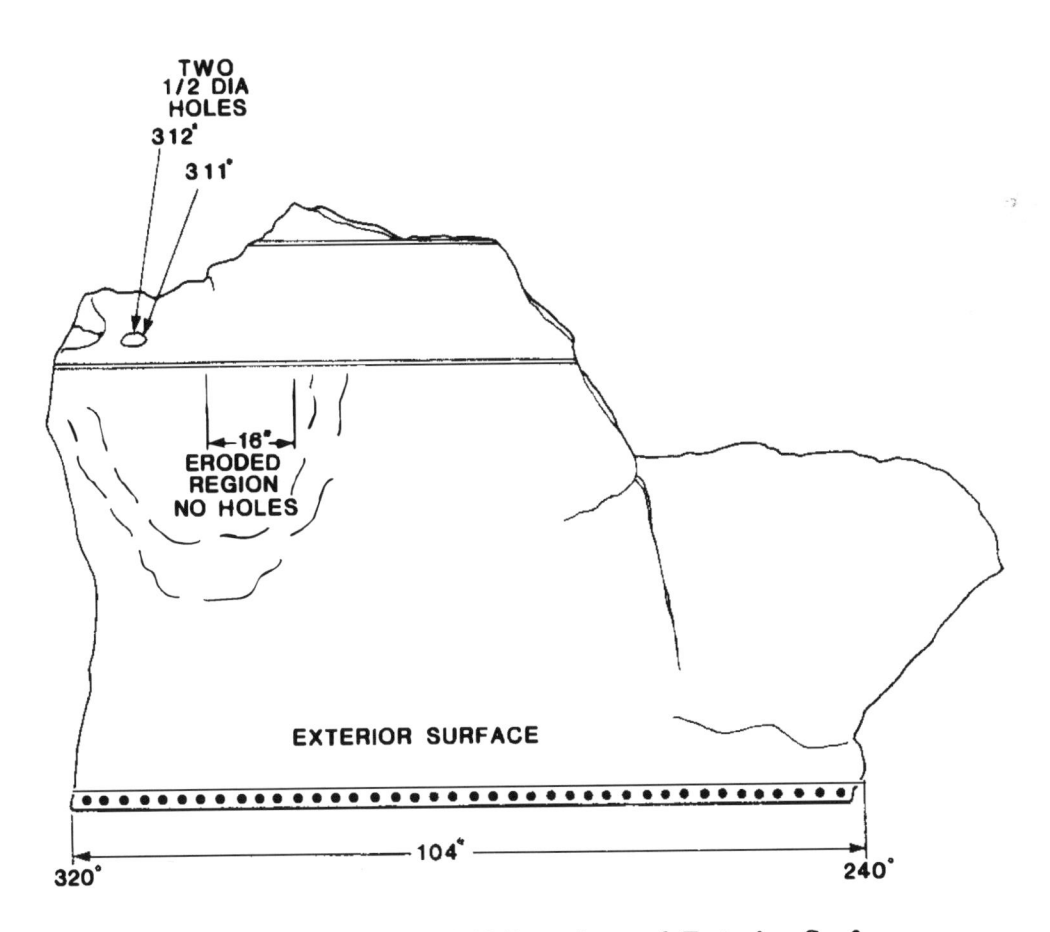

Exhibit 25. Contact #712 Interior and Exterior Surfaces

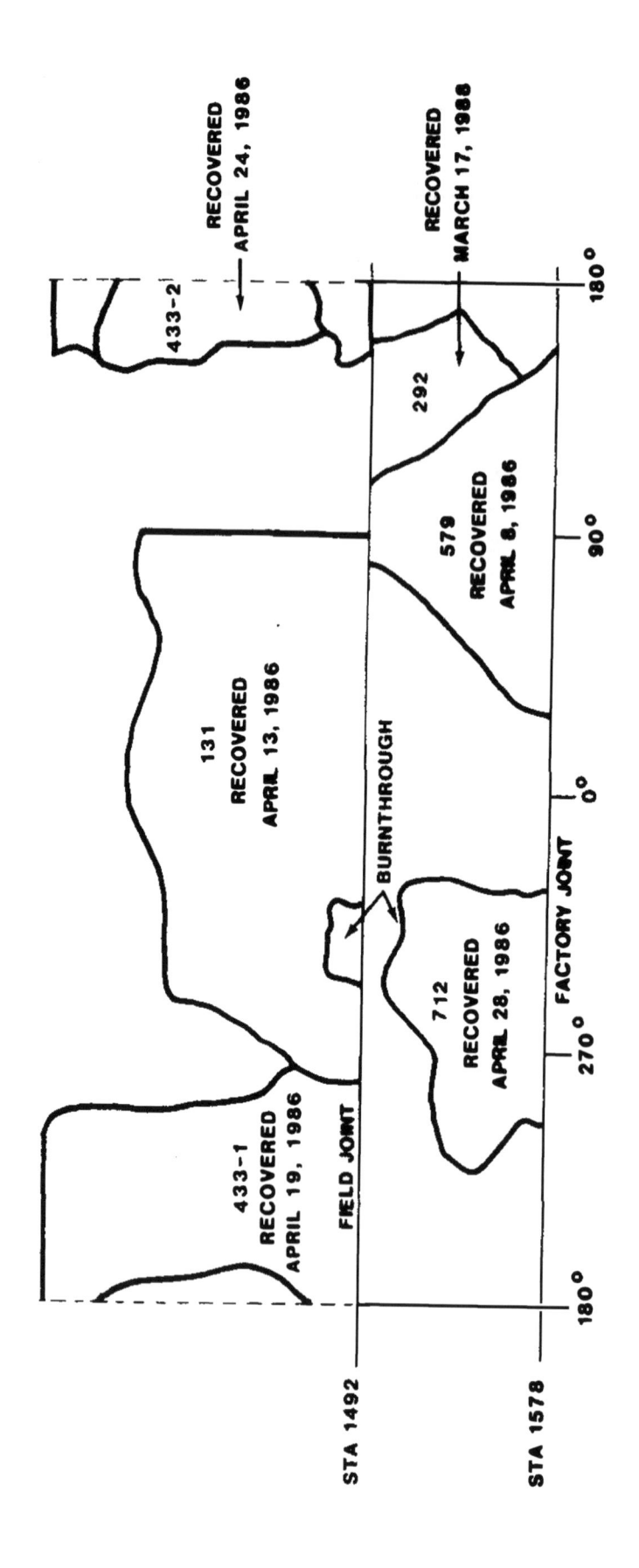

Exhibit 26. Composite of Right SRB Debris Aft Segment

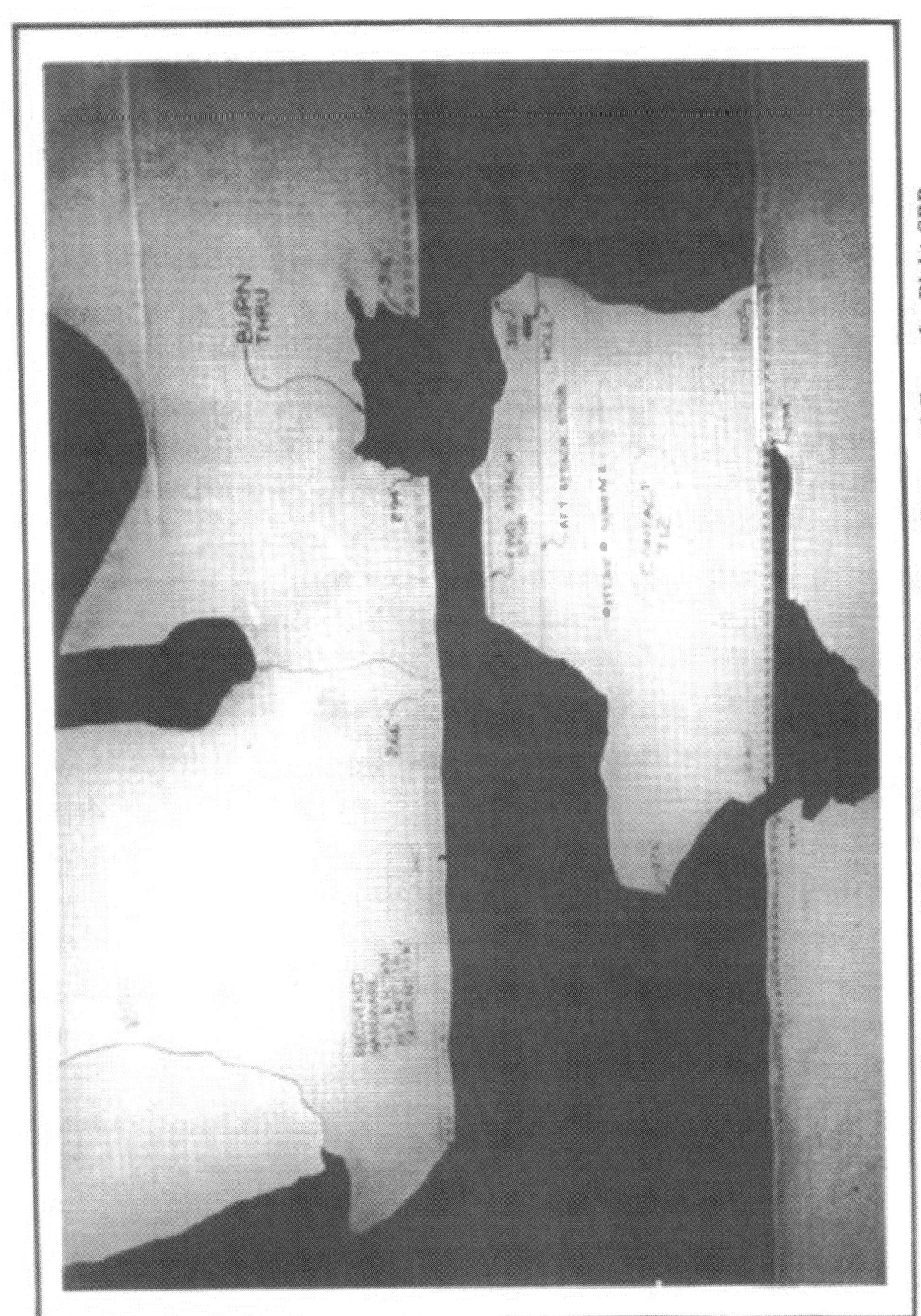

Exhibit 27. Styrofoam Full-size Composite of Major Pieces Recovered From the Right SRB

Chapter 6
CLASSIFICATION AND RECOVERY OF ORBITER AND PAYLOAD

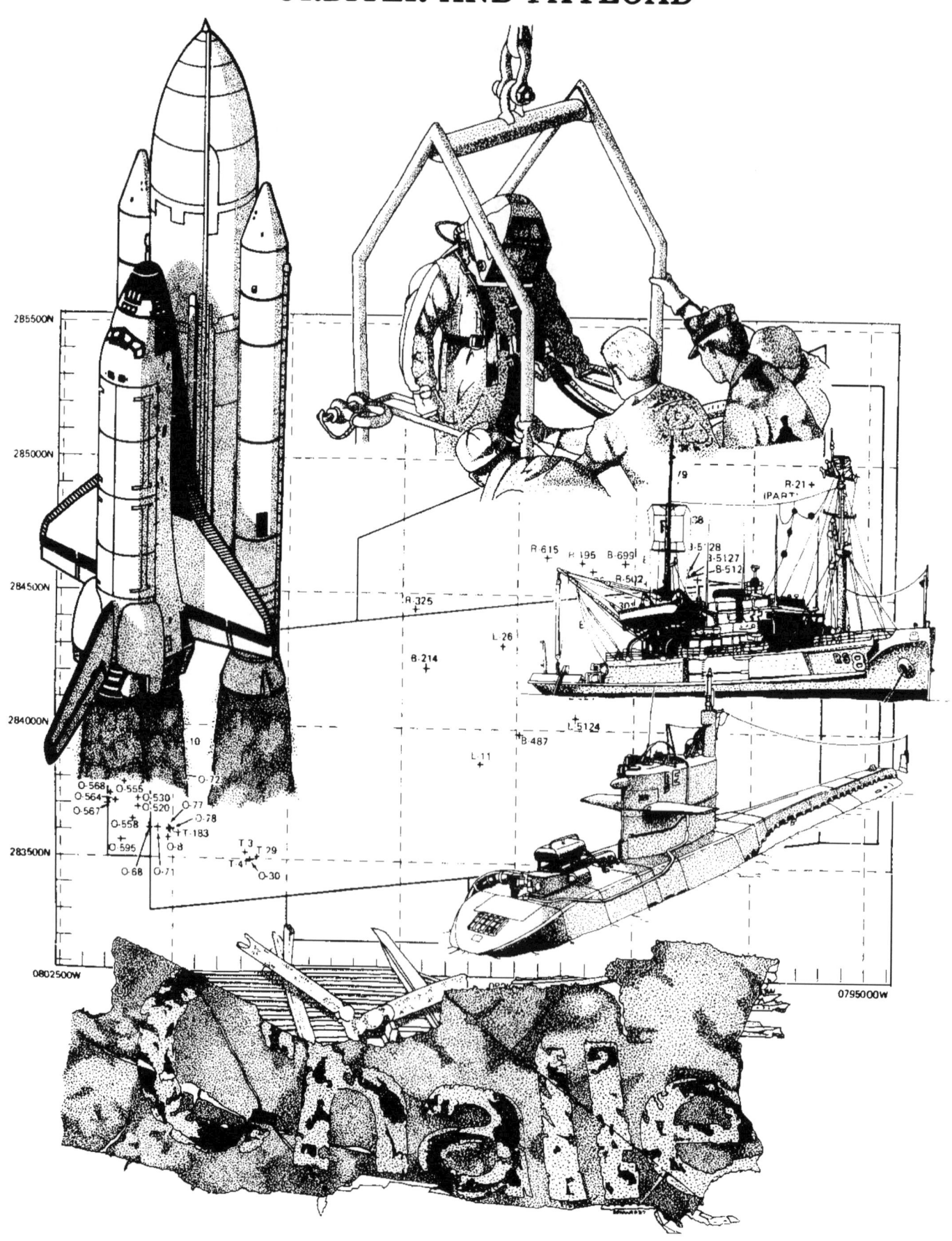

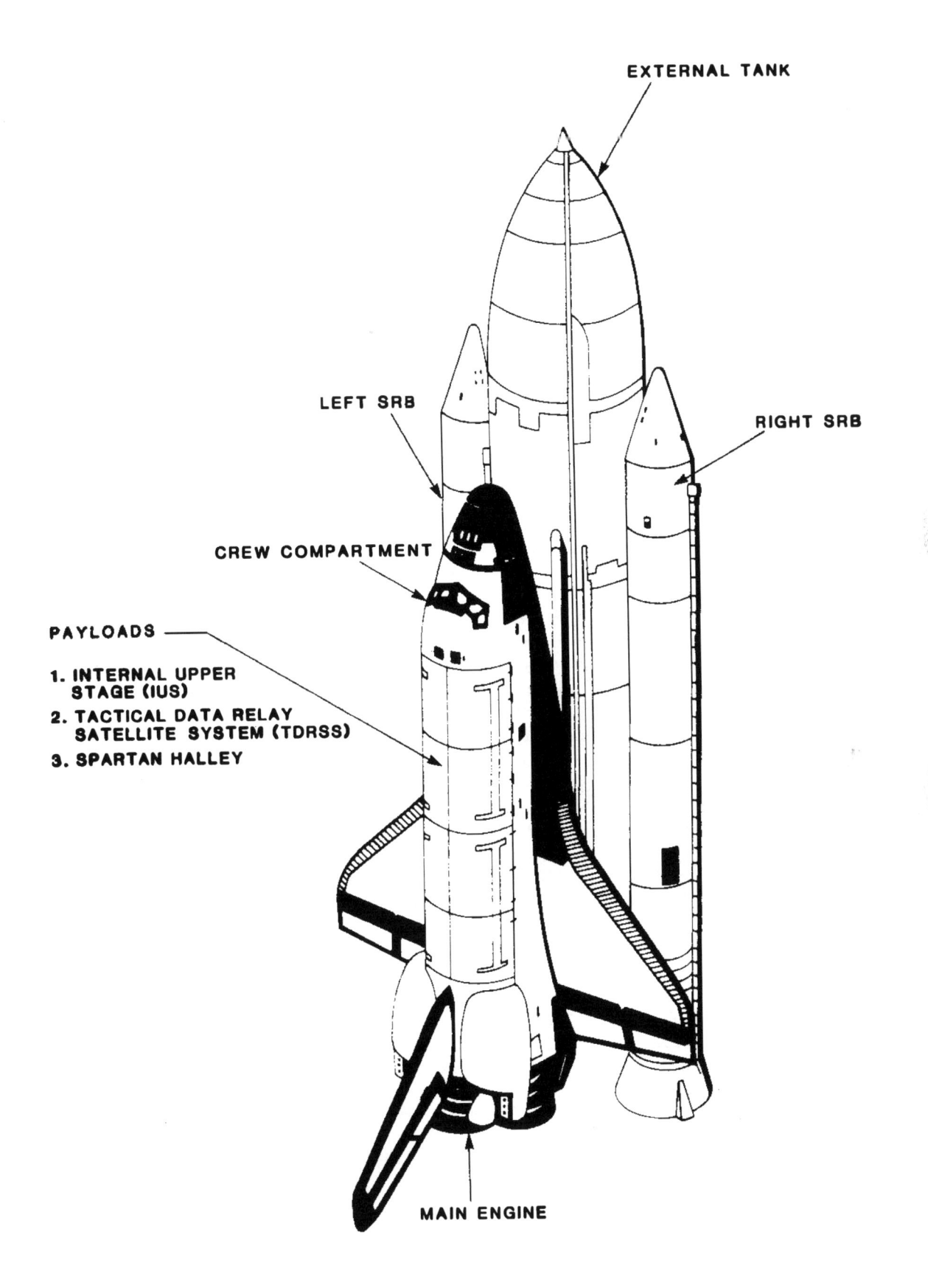

Exhibit 28. Arrangement of the Orbiter and Related Components

Chapter 6
CLASSIFICATION AND RECOVERY OF ORBITER AND PAYLOAD

6.1 Classification and Recovery. Classification and recovery operations of contacts from the STS 51-L Orbiter and its cargo continued until 29 August 1986. Exhibit 28 shows the arrangement of the Orbiter and related components. Operations were conducted mostly in shallow water in the western third of the search area and therefore used divers almost exclusively. Appendix C provides a list of recovered STS 51-L contacts. The following is a summary of Orbiter and payload components recovered:

Component	% Recovered	Volume Recovered
Orbiter	47	14,800 ft^3
External Tank	33	1,400 ft^3
Solid Rocket Boosters	50	3,600 ft^3
Payload (total)		450 ft^3
IUS	90	
TDRSS	40	
Spartan Halley	95	

6.1.2 Initial Recovery. Radar and optical data from the launch indicated that the Orbiter wreckage was scattered in the western third of the search area in nominal depths of 80 - 100 fsw (Exhibit 29). For the first 60 days, the bulk of the Orbiter salvage was conducted by USS PRESERVER (ARS 8), LCDR John Devlin commanding, which had arrived on 6 February, two days before the operation commenced. This interval was spent familiarizing key personnel and divers with space shuttle construction and detail to enhance at-sea recognition of critical and/or safety related components. This procedure was repeated throughout the operation as each new diving team arrived at KSC. The first significant debris recovered by PRESERVER proved to be from the Internal Upper Stage (IUS), a part of the CHALLENGER payload used to orbit the Tactical Data Relay Satellite System (TDRSS). From 14 to 28 February PRESERVER divers recovered debris from the Orbiter's three main engines at Contact #66.

6.1.3 Crew Compartment. The USAF LCU had been assigned to the western edge of the search area to continue localization and classification of designated sonar contacts. Finally on 7 March LCU divers classified a contact as crew compartment debris approximately 16 nm from Cape Canaveral in 100 feet of water. On 8 March Navy divers from PRESERVER reconfirmed the debris as that of the CHALLENGER crew compartment and began recovery operations in earnest. The recovery operations were hampered by weather conditions that frequently stirred up the silt-covered bottom (which reduced visibility) and by intermittent Gulf Stream eddy currents up to two knots. By 17 March divers from PRESERVER were able to recover and return to port three deck loads of crew compartment debris. PRESERVER continued recovery operations on 19 and 20 March. Poor weather conditions during the period 21 to 23 March suspended or hampered recovery operations and little progress was made. Weather and bottom conditions were again favorable on 29 March and PRESERVER continued recovery operations at the crew compartment site until 4 April when all astronaut remains and visible compartment debris had been recovered.

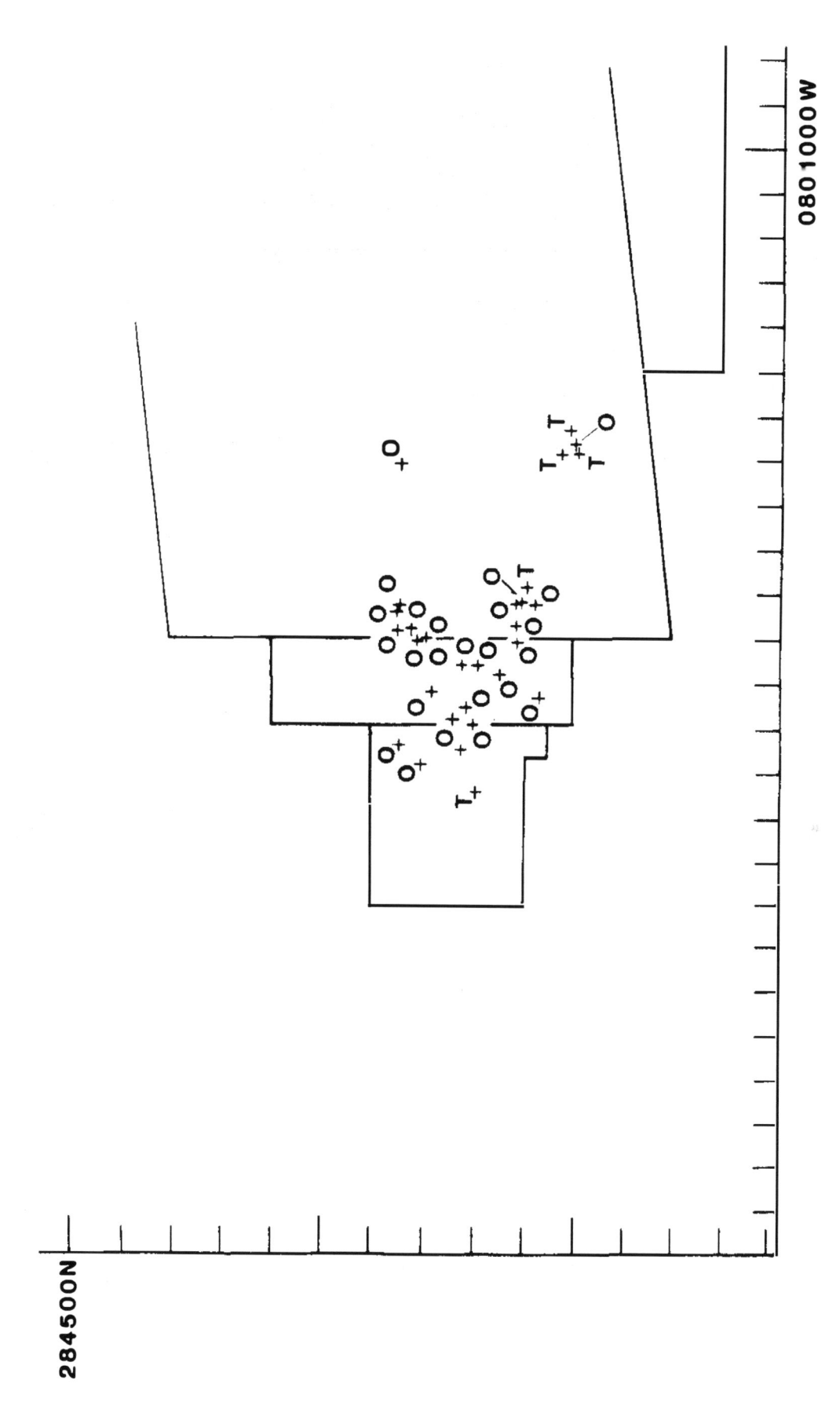

Exhibit 29. Western Edge of the Search Area

On 5 April SUPSALV contracted the scallop fishing boat, BIGFOOT, to dredge the crew compartment site for pieces of debris possibly covered by silt. This dredging operation netted additional small pieces of debris. On 7 April with improving underwater visibility SUPSALV employed EDWIN LINK with the manned submersible SEA-LINK I to videotape the crew compartment site. This survey revealed that small pieces of debris remained at the site, possibly turned up as the result of the dredging operation. From 8 to 15 April Coast Guard strike team divers operating from G.W. PIERCE II and DEEP DRONE operating from INDEPENDENCE completed the survey of the crew compartment site and the recovery of all remaining debris.

6.2 Extended Operations. After the deep water SRB phase of the salvage operation shut down on 29 April 1986, divers from the USS OPPORTUNE (LCDR M.R. Scott commanding), Mobile Diving and Salvage Unit TWO, USCG, NASA contractors and EOD Group TWO continued to work in shallow depths. The north, south and eastern limits of the Orbiter debris field had been identified through classification and recovery of Orbiter and External Tank debris. Many large pieces of the Orbiter had been recovered including the crew cabin, the right wing, most of the main engines and major pieces of fuselage. However, most of the left wing, the landing gear, most of the fuselage and cargo had not been recovered. It appeared that the debris field was larger than expected, and the remaining items of interest were outside of the established search area. A towed metal detector was mobilized onboard LIBERTY STAR and hand-held sonar, metal detectors and diver propulsion vehicles were obtained. The sonar search was expanded to the west and south and concentrated in a 52 sq nm area, shown in Exhibit 30. ESMC analysis of debris trajectories and subsequent sonar contacts supported the western shift of the search area onto Hetzel Shoal. Search classification and recovery of additional debris continued until 29 August until selected parts from almost every CHALLENGER subsystem and payload could be analyzed by NASA for detailed break-up mode determination.

6.3 Recovery Methods. To facilitate the recovery, divers utilized the combined jack-stay and circle method and the typical jack-stay search pattern to locate and retrieve debris in the shallow water areas. The specific roles of the divers and the two search methods are described in the following paragraphs.

6.3.1 Divers. Twelve dive teams consisting of 153 divers from the USN, USCG, and contractors were employed in the salvage operation. Divers were used extensively for recovery operations in shallow water areas, Exhibit 31. Both surface-supplied air and scuba diving operations were conducted. Divers proved to be effective for the recovery of debris in shallow areas where poor ocean bottom visibility often imposed an operational limitation on the use of ROV's. The ability of divers to work by feel also proved advantageous for the recovery of items in the shallow areas where visibility was frequently less than one foot. Divers used hand-held sonar and metal detectors or conducted a pattern search to locate objects or debris fields. Between 3 and 5 May a towed pulse-induction metal detector was successfully employed to define the limits of a buried debris field in a 300 square meter area of high interest. Divers with hand-held pulse-induction metal detectors were then employed to search the defined area by a combined jack-stay and circle search method. In total 3,077 dives were made in water depths to 177 feet with a cumulative bottom time of 1,549 hours. The techniques as described below were tedious but effective. In this regard the operation was analogous to typical aircraft recovery; only the area to be searched was much greater and some of the desired items were very small.

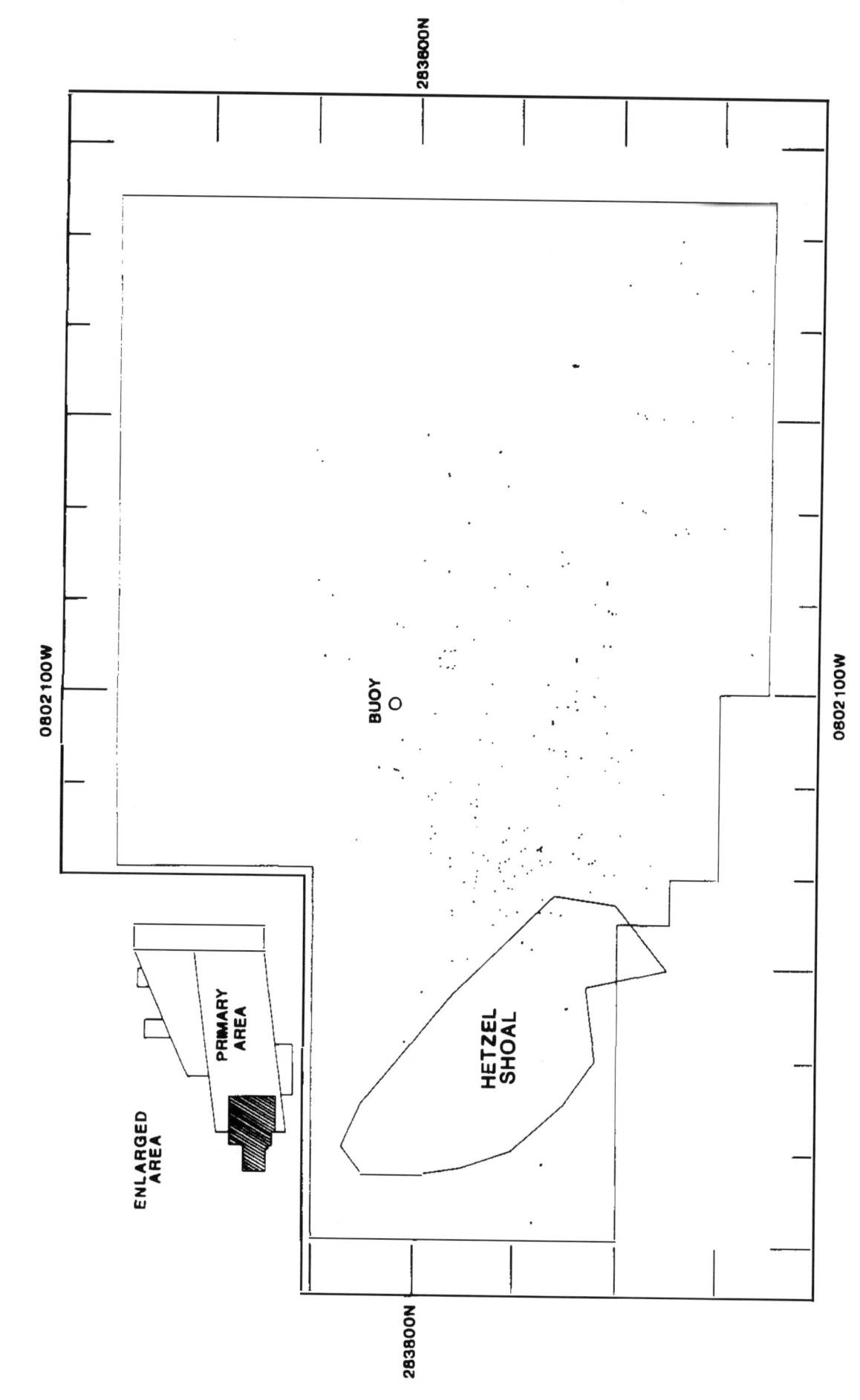

Exhibit 30. Shallow Water Search Area

Exhibit 31. Preparing to Dive from the PRESERVER

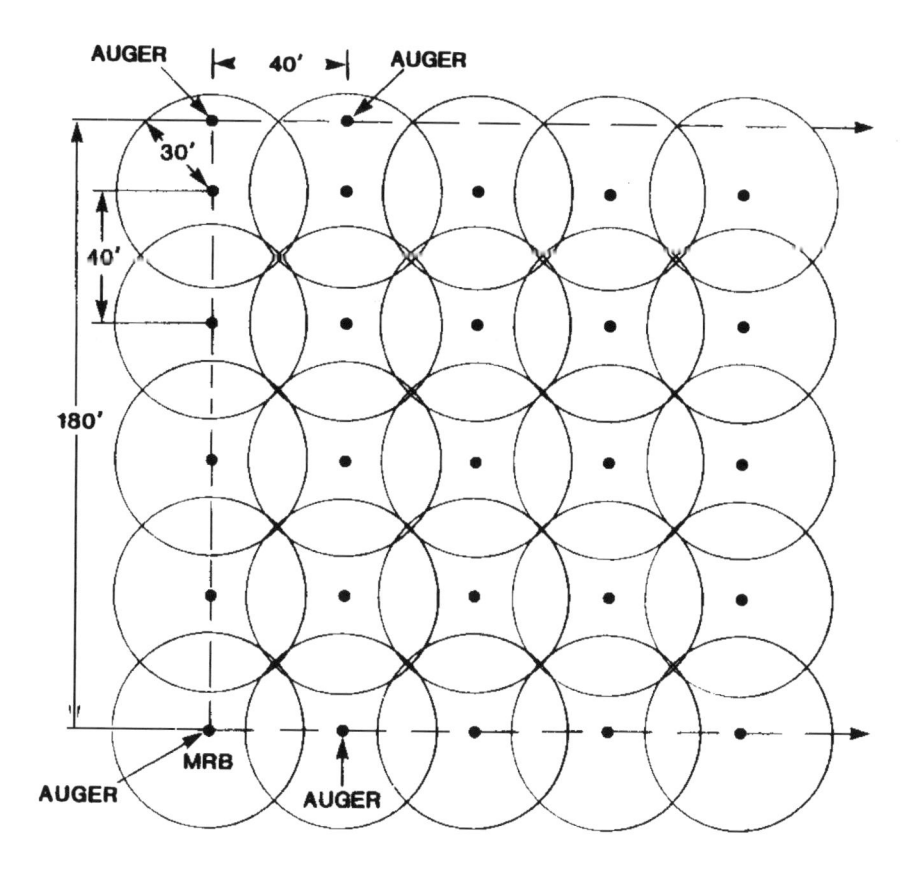

Exhibit 32. Combined Jack-stay and Circle Method

6.3.2 Combined Jack-stay Search Methods. The combined jack-stay and circle search method employed for locating buried debris with metal detectors purposely included significant overlap to eliminate the possibility of missing very small objects. Exhibit 32 shows the search pattern. A reference buoy was initially dropped on datum at the intended search area. Divers then placed an auger anchor on the sea floor at datum and established a north-south base line 180 feet long by compass swim. The base line was knotted every 40 feet and fixed at the ends with auger anchors. Similar base lines were placed parallel to the first and 40 feet apart. Divers then conducted a series of circle searches along each base line with metal detectors. Each circle had a 30-foot radius from an auger at one of the knots on the base line. Divers covered the area by searching a series of 5-foot wide concentric circles. One diver would swim the circling line around the auger while the second searched along the line with the metal detector. When a buried object was detected it was dug up and placed in a central location for recovery at the dive's end. The areas were prioritized for search by the debris pattern detected during the earlier search with a towed metal detector and visual searches of the sea floor by divers using diver propulsion vehicles.

Buried debris often presented some evidence of its location on the surface such as wires, or framing protruding above the sand. Although the protruding pieces were too small for detection by sonar, they were detectable by divers. The pulse-induction metal detectors used were able to locate small pieces of magnesium, copper and aluminum as deep as one foot beneath the sand.

6.3.3 Standard Jack-stay Search Method. A standard jack-stay search method was used by divers to visually search the bottom in selected areas for pieces of debris too small for detection by side scanning sonar. Divers also used hand-held sonar to support the search, particularly when a thermocline reduced the effectiveness of side-scanning sonar. When an area had been selected for this method of search, a reference buoy and anchor clump was dropped at datum by a surface vessel. A pattern was then laid to the four points of the compass by divers. Each leg of the pattern was 300 feet long, resulting in a 600 foot square search area divided into quarters. Exhibit 33 shows the pattern generated by a jack-stay search.

6.3.4 ROV's and Submersibles. ROV's used in the shallow water search area were at various times DEEP DRONE, SCORPI, and ASD-620. These were used mainly to speed up identification but were also used to recover Orbiter and cargo debris. They were able to process and clear contacts at a much faster rate than new contacts were identified, and quickly cleared the backlog of unidentified contacts. Because of the small size of the majority of debris items being sought from the Orbiter and payload, classification and recovery efforts were usually conducted concurrently.

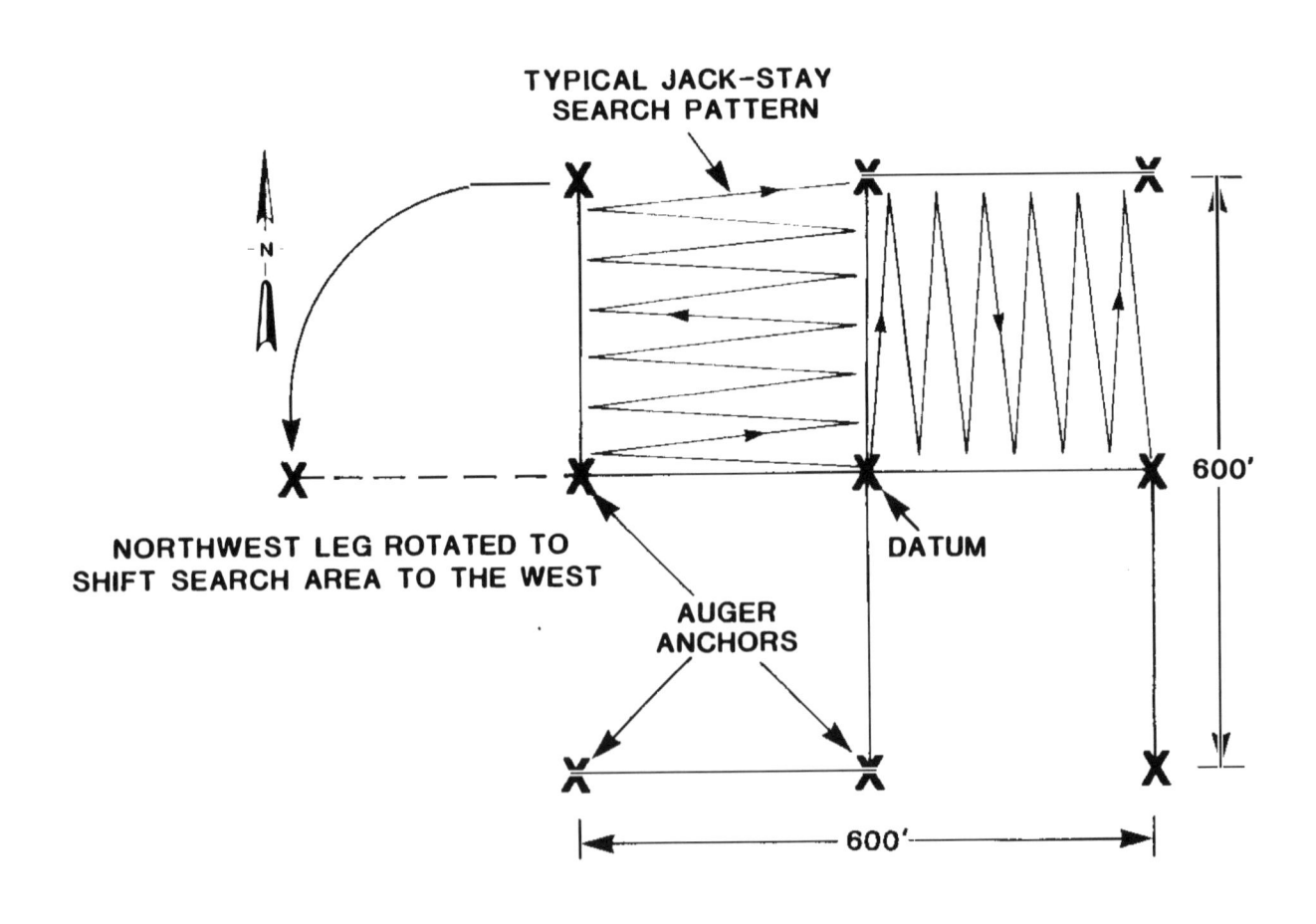

Exhibit 33. Jack-stay Search Method

6.4 Final Contact Statistics. A total of 711 designated sonar contacts were visually classified by divers, ROV's JOHNSON SEA-LINK I and II, or NR-1. Those 170 sonar contacts not classified were located in the southeastern sector of the search area where the emerging pattern of confirmed SRB locations on the sea floor indicated CHALLENGER-related debris was unlikely. The final breakdown of the classified contacts by category is as follows:

OVERALL STATISTICS

Total Number of Contacts	881
Total Investigated	711
Total Shuttle Contacts	187
Total Recovered Shuttle Contacts	167
Total Booster Contacts	48
Total Recovered Booster Contacts	35

MISCELLANEOUS INVESTIGATIONS

Other Rocketry Debris	13
Lost Aircraft	2
Shipwrecks	13
Geological Formations	256
Other Scrap and Waste	112
Nothing Found at Site	127

Chapter 7
LESSONS LEARNED

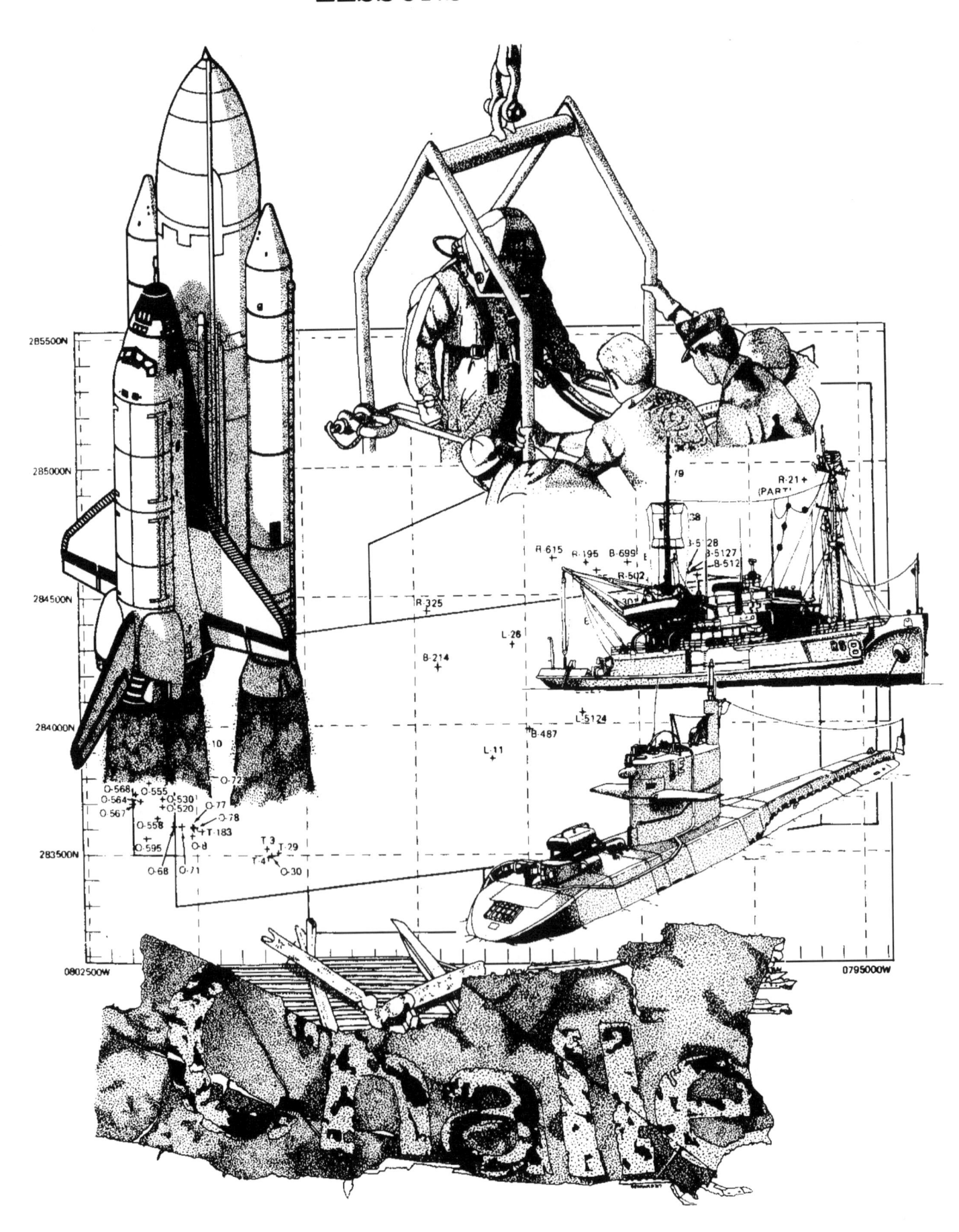

Exhibit 34. Press Conference

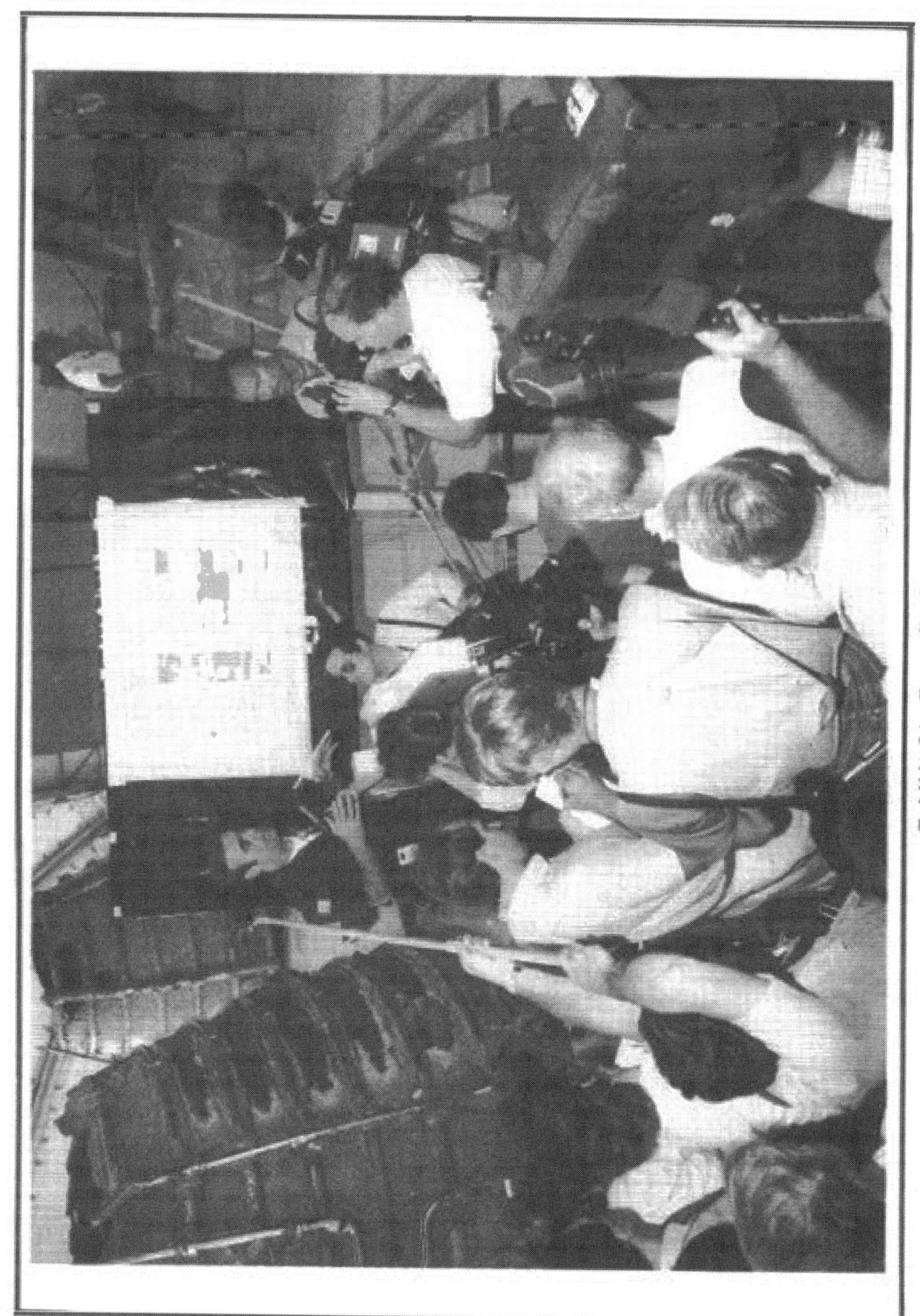

Chapter 7
LESSONS LEARNED

Lessons emerge from nearly all evolutions staged at sea and the CHALLENGER operation was no exception. This chapter summarizes those lessons which may have broad application for future salvage operations.

7.1 Command and Control. Any complex search and recovery operation requires a structured and responsive organization. Reliable, continuous communication with all units operating at sea is essential and real-time data analysis to support intelligent decision making is a critical requirement. The Navy command van complex functioned as an ad hoc Combat Information Center (CIC). All data collected at sea from the operating units and spurts of information from NASA ashore were continuously collected, compiled, analyzed and displayed. Charts and data reports were printed daily to permit enlightened decisions based upon nearly real-time information. Computerized data management and processing must be considered for any salvage operation and are mandatory for complex ones.

Normally control of operational units in the Navy is not a problem. Military units have a clear understanding of the chain of command. Similarly SUPSALV contracts contain incentives to ensure responsiveness. However unique circumstances arose in use of the NASA contractor operated vessels. Because SUPSALV exercised no military or direct contractual authority over the NASA contractor, the vessels often initially exercised "command prerogatives" and deviated from their specific orders. For example, they not infrequently "ran out of fuel" or water on Friday nights and "had" to return to port. In retrospect, firmer lines of authority should have been established with NASA at the inception to assure full compliance.

7.2 Public Affairs. When news media interest exists, the need for dedicated Navy public affairs (PA) is essential. Public affairs support from any customer agency (in this instance NASA) cannot be expected to be technically accurate nor to sufficiently promote the Navy's positive contributions. On CHALLENGER, media interest was intense. NASA PA wasn't saying much. The media turned to speculation. When a fully qualified PA Officer was provided by CHINFO, the entire PA complexion changed. Navy PA personnel then attended the daily meetings in the command vans and therefore knew the facts of the operation. They were then able to work effectively in the NASA press room and get positive Navy news released. A PA officer should always be considered as a key player when assembling a large salvage organization. In fact, the US Navy received outstanding media coverage (Exhibit 34) as a direct result of dedicated PA attention.

7.3 Navigational Accuracy of Designated Sonar Contacts. Accurate and consistent navigational systems on all ships involved with search and salvage operations is a critical requirement. The location of contacts identified during searching operations must be accurately determined so that subsequent relocation can be accomplished during classification and recovery efforts. GPS/LORAN-C was the primary navigation system used during STS 51-L search and salvage operations. This system proved to have the necessary accuracy (10 to 25 meters) to mark and then relocate identified contacts.

The locations of contacts identified during side scanning search operations proved accurate to ± 35 meters in shallow water depths and ± 100 meters in deeper water depths. These location inaccuracies can be attributed to a combination of errors induced by:

- Navigational systems
- Vortex shedding due to cross currents in the water column (stronger in deeper depths) resulting in transverse instability of the towed sonar fish
- Small variations in towing ship course, speed, and ship motion (pitch and roll) due to winds and sea state, resulting in tow cable variations and additional sonar fish relative position errors.

These contact location inaccuracies were acceptable since they were within the capabilities of ROV and manned submersible sonars and divers to relocate. In some cases, sonar contact locations were treated as discrete points when actually they are circles of probability, each with a radius of up to 1000 feet. All vessels must use identical navigation systems if even these navigational accuracies are to be achieved. Both the USAF LCU and SUNBIRD/NR-1 had installed navigation systems which were not suitable for accurate correlation with the GPS/LORAN positions.

7.4 Submarine NR-1 Utilization. SUPSALV had used the services of the submarine NR-1 on prior operations (the most notable being the recovery of an F-14 Aircraft from the USS Kennedy (CV 67) in the North Sea in 1976). However, NR-1 had never been used by SUPSALV as a search asset nor in conjunction with other conventional search and recovery vessels. As a result, two major problems emerged and were eventually overcome but which must be considered up front for any future operations involving NR-1: navigational accuracy and water management.

7.4.1 Navigational Accuracy. During the first three NR-1 missions, SUPSALV relied on the surface navigation accuracy of SUNBIRD's installed LORAN system which was subsequently found to vary markedly from the GPS/LORAN multiuser systems being employed by the other search vessels. Inherent inaccuracies in determining the position of NR-1 relative to SUNBIRD and a 150 ft/hr drift factor in the NR-1 doppler navigation system further compounded this variance. During the second NR-1 search mission several contacts had been recorded and visually classified by NR-1 as SRB, yet later when the SEA-LINK submersibles dived on the recorded coordinates they were unable to reacquire the contacts. The entire area had to be eventually re-searched by surface vessels. Subsequent efforts to correlate NR-1 and surface vessel sonar contacts disclosed variances in excess of one-half nautical mile. In multiple platform search scenarios the NR-1 support ship must be equipped with the same surface navigation system as all the other ships and inherent NR-1-to-support-ship positional errors must be updated by frequent initialization of the NR-1 doppler navigation system to the surface support ship navigation system. During the fourth and final NR-1 mission, a GPS/LORAN system was installed on SUNBIRD and navigational accuracy was sufficient to successfully perform her mission.

7.4.2 Water Management. The U.S. Navy Submarine Force enforces a rigid doctrine regarding submerged employment of submarines when other vessels in a designated operation area are using submerged devices such as side scan sonar, ROV's, manned submersibles, divers, or weighted lift lines. Large zones of separation must be maintained between the submerged submarine and other working vessels in the interest of submarine safety. During the CHALLENGER salvage operation, when as many as 13 ships were operating on independent missions at a given time throughout the entire search area, use of NR-1 required reassignment of surface assets to less desirable and less productive locations to maintain the geographic boundaries required by NR-1 for submerged operations. At times the NR-1 safety zones approached one third of the entire search area. Appendix A, Exhibit A-7 addresses this issue. During the fourth and final NR-1 mission, procedures were put in place which allowed reasonably rapid changes to the NR-1 safety boundaries, thereby reducing, but not eliminating, water management problems during NR-1 submerged operations. The lesson learned here is that water management doctrine should be a major consideration whenever NR-1 is requested to support a surface force mission. The impact of water management can vary from being no problem, to that of a minor nuisance, up to a major impediment depending upon the complexity of the particular mission.

7.5 Metal Detectors. A ship-towed, pulse-induction metal detector was effectively used by SUPSALV for the first time to locate non-ferrous debris covered by sand or silt. The unit was limited by a detection footprint of approximately six feet. Search lines were spaced about 50 feet apart. This search method allowed definition of debris field limits in high interest areas and reduction in the area subsequently searched by divers with hand-held detectors. Hand-held, pulse-induction metal detectors were effectively used by divers to locate buried non-ferrous debris including magnesium, aluminum, beryllium, copper and titanium. The process was slow and tedious but very successful. Divers with no previous experience in the use of this equipment quickly learned to use metal detectors effectively.

7.6 ROV's Versus Manned Submersibles. ROV's selected for employment in the Gulf Stream at deep depths or in other high current areas must be capable of overcoming the effects of current drag on the support cable. The GEMINI proved capable of operating in this environment while the DEEP DRONE did not. Unlike the DEEP DRONE, which uses a direct ship-to-vehicle cable, the GEMINI was used with a Tether Management Assembly (TMA). One ROV support cable connects from the ship to the weighted TMA, and a second umbilical cable connects from the TMA to the ROV. The heavy TMA could be lowered to a position near the bottom, which allowed the GEMINI to pull around only a short tether in the slower bottom currents. GEMINI was able to work in areas with as much as three to four knots of surface current whereas the DEEP DRONE could not.

The SEA-LINK submersibles were also extremely effective in working in the eastern portions of the search area. In fact their capabilities complemented those of GEMINI very nicely. They were more mobile and could locate and attach a lifting pendant to the target more rapidly than GEMINI. On the other hand each submersible had a nominal eight hour working day whereas GEMINI could work 24 hours a day if required.

Perhaps the single biggest advantage of ROV's is elimination of the element of underwater personnel safety. An excellent example occurred when the GEMINI TMA was under repair and SUPSALV attempted to use a SEA-LINK submersible to attach the lifting line to the installed pendant on a high priority SRB segment. Because Harbor Branch Foundation management prudently did not want to expose their submersible to danger should the STENA WORKHORSE lose dynamic positioning and possibly drag the lift line and clump across the submersible during the attachment process, it was decided to buoy off the lift line so STENA could clear the area while the SEA-LINK made the attachment. The attachment process was unsuccessful when the lift line/clump was found to have been dragged over a mile away by the strong Gulf Stream surface currents. Further attempts were abandoned. The lesson learned here is more judgement than fact. Both ROV's and manned submersibles possess relative advantages and disadvantages. Deep diving manned submersibles are normally installed on a permanent support ship whereas ROV's can normally be air shipped on short notice anywhere in the world by C-141 aircraft, and then be operated from a vessel of opportunity. Normally SUPSALV prefers ROV's for working on the sea floor because of these human safety and mobility considerations. However on CHALLENGER, when large quantities of assets were needed, manned submersibles were chartered and safely used with extreme effectiveness.

7.7 Dynamic Positioning. Ship, ROV and personnel operational time in both shallow and deep water operations are markedly reduced if vessels are provided with a dynamic positioning capability. This was apparent on STENA WORKHORSE, where she could maintain station on dynamic positioning even in heavy weather and easily position her lift lines adjacent to the SRB targets. While a conventional static mooring may be attractive in a single, shallow debris field, it would simply not have worked on CHALLENGER due to the large numbers of deep, geographically separated work sites.

7.8 Sonar for Direct Diver Support. In a heavy work environment in relatively shallow water, divers are extremely efficient compared to ROV's or other sophisticated assets. However, as water depth increases or the worksite becomes increasingly dispersed, divers become less effective because they must use greater percentages of their more limited bottom time to locate the particular work target. This problem is typical in aircraft recovery operations where debris fields can be extensive. On CHALLENGER, UDI and Mesotech sonars were plumbed beneath the support ships to assist divers by vectoring them to potential targets with varying degrees of success. Later on the SCORPI and ASD 620 ROV's were used with even more effectiveness because they could readily locate the target and, if recovery was required, the divers could immediately locate same by following the ROV umbilical. This procedure leads to a potential requirement for a low cost, 300 fsw lightweight ROV specifically configured to work with divers.

Chapter 8
CONCLUSIONS

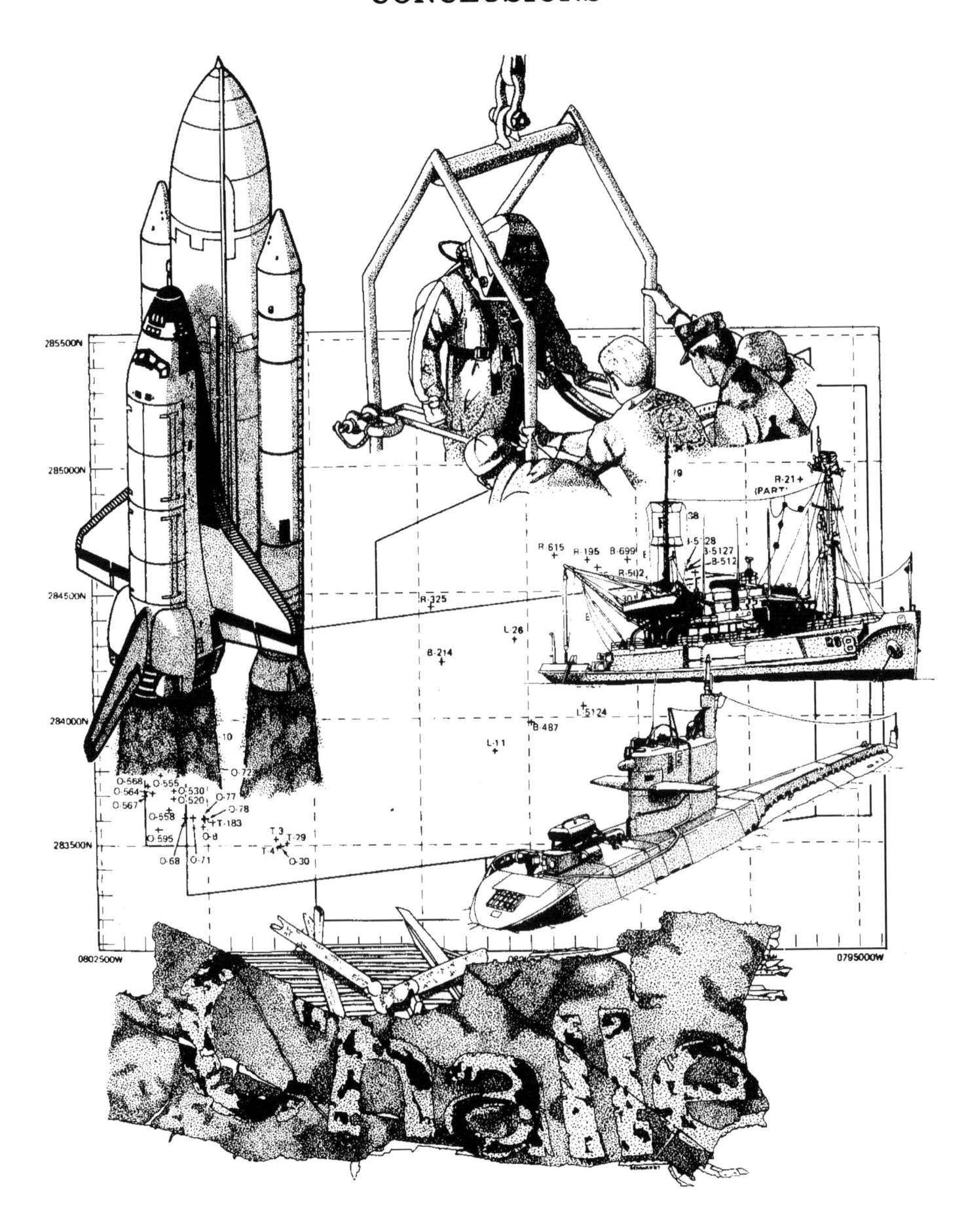

Exhibit 35. CHALLENGER Liftoff

Chapter 8
CONCLUSIONS

The text of this report is of necessity filled with charts, statistics, hardware specifications, technical procedure and wiring diagrams. However, as is always the case, it is the people who get things done and make all the hardware and procedural doctrine work. Throughout the seven-month CHALLENGER salvage operation, and in particular during the first three months, the salvage personnel all demonstrated the professionalism which we in the Navy tend to take for granted. All NASA objectives were met or exceeded. The Navy diving and salvage community's role in helping the nation's space program get back in the air (Exhibit 35) was complete. Appendix A, Exhibits A-8 and A-9 address these commendable accomplishments.

REFERENCES

1. "Dealing with Disaster," LCDR Deborah A. Burnette, USN, Military Media Review, October 1986, pp. 23-29.

2. "Probing the Deep for CHALLENGER Disaster Answers," Sea Technology, May 1986, pp 37-42.

3. "Picking up the Pieces," All Hands, June 1986, pp 18-22.

4. USS SUNBIRD (ARS 15) letter 4740 ser 86 of 19 April 1986.

5. Submarine NR-1 letter 4740 ser 80-86 of 5 May 1986.

6. USS PRESERVER (ARS 8) letter 4740 ser 121-86 of 16 May 1986.

7. USS KITTIWAKE (ARS 13) letter 3504 ser DECK/200 of 19 May 1986.

8. USS OPPORTUNE (ARS 41) letter 4700 of 4 June 1986.

9. Mission 51-L Salvage Operation - Search, Classification and Recovery Supervisor of Salvage, NAVSEA, September 26, 1986 (general).

10. "Space Shuttle CHALLENGER Search and Recovery Operations, February - August 1986," Tracor Marine, Inc.

11. "The CHALLENGER Space Shuttle Investigation," Eastport International, Inc.

12. "Final Report for STS 51-L CHALLENGER Searchops, Cape Canaveral, Florida," Steadfast Oceaneering, Inc.

13. "Report of the Presidential Commission on the Space Shuttle CHALLENGER Accident," Vol. III, Appendix O, NASA Search Recovery & Reconstruction Task Force Team Report.

Appendix A
NAVAL MESSAGES

UNCLASSIFIED   EXHIBIT A-1

IMMEDIATE PRIORITY

O P 311045Z JAN 86

FM DOD MGRS STS CONTINGENCY SPT OFC PAFB FL//DDMS O//

TO CNO WASH DC

INFO COMNAVSEASYSCOM WASH DC   CINCLANTFLT NORFOLK VA
COMNAVSURFLANT NORFOLK VA   JCS WASH DC//J3/J34/J36/J5//
DOD MGR STS CONTINGENCY SPT OPS PETERSON AFB CO//DO/DDM
    S DD//
JSC HOUSTON TX//TM2 DDMS//   NASA KSC PAFB FL//EX NAMO//

UNCLAS //N04740//

SUBJ; SALVAGE SUPPORT FOR STS 51-L MISHAP.

1. FOR OP-642C3.

2. NASA HAS REQUESTED THE DOD PROVIDE SALVAGE SERVICES IN SUPPORT OF THE STS 51-L ACCIDENT INVESTIGATION BOARD.

3. REQUEST NAVY ASSISTANCE FOR THIS EFFORT.

4. FUNDING CITATIONS WILL BE PROVIDED BY SEPARATE CORRESPONDENCE.

5. DDMS POINT OF CONTACT IS LCDR SHULTZ, AV 854-5116.

BT

00C(2) . . . INFO FOR COMNAVSEASYSCOM WASH(5)   15709/ 3/1671
PMS395(1) 00(1) 09B352(1)

                                                        RTD:052-000/COPIES:0005

266297/031   1 OF 1   MATA2105 031/16:08Z   311045Z JAN 86
CSN:AUIB02461   DOD MGRS STS C

UNCLASSIFIED

UNCLASSIFIED

IMMEDIATE PRIORITY

O P 312234Z JAN 86

FM CNO WASHINGTON DC

TO COMNAVSEASYSCOM WASHINGTON DC   CINCLANTFLT NORFOLK VA

INFO JCS WASHINGTON DC   CINCPACFLT PEARL HARBOR HI
COMNAVSURFLANT NORFOLK VA   COMNAVAIRLANT NORFOLK VA
JSC HOUSTON TX   NASA KSC PAFB FL
DOD MGR STS CONTINGENCY SPT OFC PAFB FL
DOD MGR STS CONTINGENCY SPT OPS PETERSON AFB CO

UNCLAS //N04740//

SUBJ; SALVAGE SUPPORT FOR STS 51-L MISHAP

A. DOD MGRS STS CONTINGENCY SPT OFC PAFB FL 311045Z JAN 86 PASEP

1. FOR COMNAVSEASYSCOM. TAKE REF A FORAC, DIRLAUTH TO PROVIDE MOST EXPEDITIOUS AND APPROPRIATE USN/COMMERCIAL ASSETS.

2. FOR CINCLANTFLT. PROVIDE SEARCH AND RECOVERY ASSETS AS FEASIBLE IN SUPPORT OF SALVAGE EFFORTS.

3. OPNAV POC LCDR C. BREWER, A/V 225-1150.

BT

00C(2) ... ACT FOR COMNAVSEASYSCOM WASH(5)   15709/ 3/1671
   PMS395(1) 00(1) 09B352(1)

                                                RTD:000-000/COPIES:0005

268822/031   1 OF 1   MATA3039 031/23:10Z   312234Z JAN 86
CSN:AUIA02445   CNO WASHINGTON

UNCLASSIFIED

```
UUUUUUUUUUUUUUUUUUUUUUUUUUUUUU
U   U N C L A S S I F I E D   U
UUUUUUUUUUUUUUUUUUUUUUUUUUUUUU
```

IMMEDIATE

O 010155Z FEB 86

FM COMNAVSEASYSCOM WASHINGTON DC

TO CINCLANTFLT NORFOLK VA   COMNAVSURFLANT NORFOLK VA

INFO CNO WASHINGTON DC   JCS WASHINGTON DC
CINCPACFLT PEARL HARBOR HI   COMNAVAIRLANT NORFOLK VA
COMSUBLANT NORFOLK VA   COMSERVGRU TWO
COMSERVRON EIGHT   CAPE CANAVERAL AFS FL//CC//
DDMS-O PATRICK AFB FL   ESMC PATRICK AFB FL//R05//
NASA KSC FL//SF-SEC-UA//

UNCLAS //N04740//

SUBJ; NASA SPACE SHUTTLE UNDERWATER SEARCH & SALVAGE

A. DDMS-O PATRICK AFB FL 311545Z JAN 86
B. CNO WASHINGTON DC 312234Z JAN 86
C. PHONCON COMNAVSEASYSCOM (CODE 00C) CAPT BARTHOLOMEW/
/CINCLANTFLT LCDR CHAMBERLAIN OF 31 JAN 86
D. PHONCON COMNAVSEASYSCOM (CODE 00C) CAPT BARTHOLOMEW/
COMNAVSURFLANT CDR WHALL OF 31 JAN 86

1. PER REFS A & B, ORIG TASKED TO LOCATE AND SALVAGE UNDERWATER WRECKAGE OF SPACE SHUTTLE CHALLENGER AND BOTH SOLID ROCKET BOOSTERS (SRB'S). EFFORTS ONGOING AT THIS TIME TO REFINE SEARCH AREA(S) IN ANTICIPATION OF 60-100 DAY SEARCH/SALVAGE OPERATION UTILIZING BOTH FLEET & NAVSEA CONTRACTOR ASSETS.

2. SUBJECT TO CONTINUING REFINEMENT, SEARCH AREA IN EXCESS OF 600 SQ MI WITH WATER DEPTHS DOWN TO 1300 FSW. WHILE BOTTOM TOPOGRAPHY APPEARS FAVORABLE FOR SONAR SEARCH, GULF STREAM CURRENTS MAY BE MAJOR FACTOR IN SALVOPS, PRELIMINARY SEARCH/SALVAGE PLAN FOLLOWS:
  A.   SUPSALV WILL PROVIDE OVERALL TECHNICAL DIRECTION AND WILL

00C(2)... ORIG FOR COMNAVSEASYSCOM WASH(5)   15709/15/1671
00CBC(1) 00C2S052(1) 09B3341(1)

RTD:034-000/COPIES:0005

270607/032   1 OF 2   MATA0 74 032/03:07Z   010155Z FEB 86
CSN:VDTC00034   COMNAVSEASYSCO

```
UUUUUUUUUUUUUUUUUUUUUUUUUUUUUU
U   U N C L A S S I F I E D   U
UUUUUUUUUUUUUUUUUUUUUUUUUUUUUU
```

UUUUUUUUUUUUUUUUUUUUUUUUUUUUUUUU
U   U N C L A S S I F I E D   U
UUUUUUUUUUUUUUUUUUUUUUUUUUUUUUUU

SET UP OPCON CENTER TO BE MANNED FULL TIME BY SUPSALV, SEARCH SPECIALISTS AND LOGISTIC SUPPORT PERSONNEL.

    B.   NAVSEA CONTRACT PERSONNEL WILL SET UP MULTI-USER PRECISE NAV SYSTEM.

    C.   PRELIMINARY SEARCH WILL BE CONDUCTED FROM NASA SRB RETRIEVAL VESSELS M/V LIBERTY AND M/V FREEDOM MANNED BY NAVSEA CONTRACT SEARCH TEAMS TO CONDUCT PRECISION SIDE SCAN SONAR SEARCH OF ENTIRE AREA. ONE VESSEL WILL BE EQUIPPED FOR DEEP WATER SEARCH IN EXCESS OF 1500 FSW. SCORPIO ROV WILL ALSO BE EMBARKED.

    D.   CONFIRMING REFS C & D, REQ LANTFLT SUPPORT FOR SALVOPS. INTENTIONS WOULD BE TO ASSIGN HIGHEST PROBABILITY SEARCH AREAS TO AVAILABLE FLEET ASSETS HAVING SONAR SEARCH AND AIR DIVING CAPABILITY. MIXED GAS DIVING CAPABILITY MAY BE REQUIRED LATER DEPENDENT UPON ACTUAL WRECKAGE DEPTH.

    E.   ASSETS REQUIRED FOR SALVAGE OF WRECKAGE CAN VARY GREATLY DEPENDENT UPON WATER DEPTH, CURRENT, BOTTOM TOPOGRAPHY AND OBJECT WEIGHT(S), ORIG IN PROCESS OF IDENTIFYING AND/OR STAGING ANTICIPATED UNIQUE SALVAGE ASSETS TO COMPLEMENT THOSE ALREADY PLANNED TO BE ON SCENE WITH SEARCH TEAMS.

3. EXPENDITURE OF NON-DON SALVAGE FUNDS AUTHORIZED.

BT

UNCLASSIFIED EXHIBIT A-4

PRIORITY

P 061717Z FEB 86

FM COMNAVSEASYSCOM WASHINGTON DC

TO CINCLANTFLT NORFOLK VA

INFO CNO WASHINGTON DC COMNAVSURFALNT NORFOLK VA
COMSUBLANT NORFOLK VA COMSERVRON EIGHT
DDMS SOC PATRICK AFB FL CCFS FL//CC//
ESMC PATRICK AFB FL//R05// NASA KSC-NTS PAFB FL//SF-SEC-UA//
SUBMARINE NR ONE COMSUBRON TWO
COMSUBGRU TWO USS SUNBIRD
NAVORDTESTU CAPE CANAVERAL FL//SPP40//

UNCLAS //N04740//

SUBJ; SPACE SHUTTLE CHALLENGER RECOVERY OPS

A. CNO WASHINGTON DC 312234Z JAN 86 (NOTAL)

1. AS PER TASKING REF A, REQ PROVIDE NR-1 FOR A THREE WEEK PERIOD ON-SCENE IN SUPPORT OF SUBJ OPS. REQUEST PROJECTED ARRIVAL DATE.

2. EXPENDITURE OF NON-DON SALVAGE FUNDS AUTHORIZED FOR TAD AND OTHER OUT-OF-COSTS.

BT

00C21(2)... ORIG FOR COMNAVSEASYSCOM WASH(8) 14638/15/1215
 00C3(1) 00C(1) 00C5S067(1) 09B3341(1) 08(1) 395(1)

RTD;034-000/COPIES:0008

304793/037 1 OF 1 MATA0378 037/22:26Z 061717Z FEB 86
CSN:VDTC00152 COMNAVSEASYSCO

```
UUUUUUUUUUUUUUUUUUUUUUUUUUUUUUU
U   U N C L A S S I F I E D   U
UUUUUUUUUUUUUUUUUUUUUUUUUUUUUUU
```

ADMINISTRATIVE MESSAGE

PRIORITY

P 121809Z MAR 86 ZYB

FM COMNAVSEASYSCOM WASHINGTON DC

TO CINCLANTFLT NORFOLK VA

INFO CNO WASHINGTON DC   COMSUBLANT NORFOLK VA
COMNAVSURFLANT NORFOLK VA   COMSUBRON SIX
COMSUBGRU SIX   USS KITTIWAKE
DDMS SOC PATRICK AFB FL

UNCLAS //N04740//

SUBJ; SPACE SHUTTLE CHALLENGER SALVOPS

A. CNO WASHINGTON DC 312234Z JAN 86 (NOTAL)
B. COMNAVSEASYSCOM WASHINGTON DC 010155Z FEB 86 (NOTAL)

1. SUBJ OPS INITIATED REFS A AND B CONTINUE. TO DATE APPROX 400 SONAR CONTACTS IDENTIFIED WHICH REQUIRE VISUAL CLASSIFICATION AS PREREQUISITE TO INITIATION OF RECOVERY OPS. APPROX 50 OF THESE CONTACTS IN 150-300 FSW PRESENTLY REQUIRE CLASSIFICATION AND POSSIBLE RECOVERY ON PRIORITY BASIS. UTILIZATION OF USS SUNBIRD MIXED GAS DIVING CAPABILITY CONSTRAINED DUE COMMITMENT TO SUPPORT NRI SUBMERGED OPS.

2. PER PARA 2D REF B, REQ ADVISE AVAILABILITY OF USS KITTIWAKE TO SUPPORT SUBJ OPS UPON COMPLETION ONGOING USAF F-16 SALVOPS OR OF OTHER MIXED GAS DIVING CAPABLE ASSET.

BT

00C(1) . . . ORIG FOR COMNAVSEASYSCOM WASH(3)   /13/
  00CS0146(1) 09B4311(1)

                                                      RTD;000-000/COPIES:0003

510966/071   1 OF 1   MATA2908 071/20;29Z   121809Z MAR 86
CSN:OCIA00110   COMNAVSEASYSCO

```
UUUUUUUUUUUUUUUUUUUUUUUUUUUUUUU
U   U N C L A S S I F I E D   U
UUUUUUUUUUUUUUUUUUUUUUUUUUUUUUU
```

```
UUUUUUUUUUUUUUUUUUUUUUUUUUUUUUU      EXHIBIT A-6
U    U N C L A S S I F I E D     U
UUUUUUUUUUUUUUUUUUUUUUUUUUUUUUU
```

IMMEDIATE

O 212025Z MAR 86

FM COMNAVSEASYSCOM WASHINGTON DC

TO CINCLANTFLT NORFOLK VA

INFO CNO WASHINGTON DC	COMSUBLANT NORFOLK VA
COMNAVSURFLANT NORFOLK VA	COMSUBGRU TWO
COMSUBGRU SIX	COMSUBRON TWO
USS SUNBIRD	SUBMARINE NR ONE
NAVORDTESTU CAPE CANAVERAL FL	DDMS SOC PATRICK AFB FL

UNCLAS //N04740//

SUBJ: SPACE SHUTTLE CHALLENGER SALVOPS

A. COMNAVSEASYSCOM WASHINGTON DC 061717Z FEB 86 (NOTAL)

1. LARGE AREA SEARCH PHASE OF SUBJ OPS NEARING COMPLETION. IN EXCESS OF 500 SONAR CONTACTS LOGGED OF WHICH APPROX 150 ARE IN HIGH PROB AREA FOR RIGHT AND LEFT SRB'S. IN VIEW OF MAGNITUDE OF EFFORT TO VISUALLY CLASSIFY EA SONAR CONTACT, UNIQUE CAPABILITIES OF NR1 FOR RAPID TARGET CLASSIFICATION CONSIDERED CRITICAL TO TIMELY RECOVERY OF KEY SRB COMPONENTS. THEREFORE, REQ EXTENSION OF REF A NR1 SERVICES WITH SHIP ARRIVAL PORT CANAVERAL 26 MAR 86 OR AS SOON THEREAFTER AS POSSIBLE FOR APPROX 2-3 WKS.

BT

00C(1)... ORIG FOR COMNAVSEASYSCOM WASH(5)   /13/
  00CSC020(1) PMS395(1) 08(1) 09B4311(1)

                                                RTD;000-031/COPIES:0005

571523/080   1 OF 1   MATA2629 080/20;36Z   212025Z MAR 86
CSN:OCIA00108   COMNAVSEASYSCO

```
UUUUUUUUUUUUUUUUUUUUUUUUUUUUUUU        EXHIBIT A-7
U   U N C L A S S I F I E D   U
UUUUUUUUUUUUUUUUUUUUUUUUUUUUUUU
```

PRIORITY

P 282006Z FEB 86

FM COMNAVSEASYSCOM WASHINGTON DC

TO CNO WASHINGTON DC   CINCLANTFLT NORFOLK VA

INFO COMSUBLANT NORFOLK VA   COMNAVSURFLANT NORFOLK VA
COMSUBGRU SIX   COMSUBGRU TWO
USS SUNBIRD   SUBMARINE NR ONE
NAVORDTESTU CAPE CANAVERAL FL   COMSUBRON TWO
DOD MGRS STS CONTINGENCY SPT OFC PATRICK AFB FL
  //DDMS-O//

UNCLAS //N04740//

SUBJ: SPACE SHUTTLE CHALLENGER SALVOPS

A. COMSUBRON TWO 191750Z FEB 86 (NOTAL)
B. PHONCON COMNAVSEASYSCOM CAPT BARTHOLOMEW/COMSUBRON TWO CDR

   DOLAN OF 27 FEB 86

C. PHONCON COMNAVSEASYSCOM CAPT BARTHOLOMEW/COMSUBLANT

   CAPT CAMILLERI OF 28 FEB 86

1. REF A AMENDED COMSUBRON TWO OP ORDER TO PARTITION CHALLENGER SEARCH AREA INTO THREE SECTORS SUCH THAT WHEN NR1 SUBMERGED OPS ARE IN PROGRESS, NO OTHER SEARCH OR SALVAGE ASSET MAY WORK IN THAT SECTOR.

2. ALL PRESENT AND PLANNED NR1 OPS ARE IN THE EASTERNMOST SECTOR (BOUNDED TO THE WEST BY LN 079 59WO) WHICH CONTAINS THE HIGHEST PROB AREAS FOR RECOVERY OF THE CRITICAL PORTIONS OF BOTH SRBS.

3. ANTICIPATE URGENCY OF SITUATION WILL REQUIRE CONDUCT OF SIMULTANEOUS OPS IN THIS 110 SQ NM SECTOR. REFS B & C REQUESTS TO SUBDIVIDE EASTERN SECTOR INTO SMALLER AREAS TO PERMIT SIMULTANEOUS WORK ON MULTIPLE TARGETS DISAPPROVED DUE SUBMARINE SAFETY CONSIDERATIONS.

00CB(1) . . . ORIG FOR COMNAVSEASYSCOM WASH(8)   /13/
  00C2(1) 00C(1) 00C2S115(1) PMS395(1) SEA92(1) SEA08(1) 09B3341(1)

                                              RTD:000-000/COPIES:0008

  438288/059   1 OF 2   MATA3053 059/22:48Z   282006Z FEB 86
  CSN:0CIB00208   COMNAVSEASYSCO

```
UUUUUUUUUUUUUUUUUUUUUUUUUUUUUUU
U   U N C L A S S I F I E D   U
UUUUUUUUUUUUUUUUUUUUUUUUUUUUUUU
```

```
UUUUUUUUUUUUUUUUUUUUUUUUUUUUUUUU     EXHIBIT A-7
U     U N C L A S S I F I E D     U
UUUUUUUUUUUUUUUUUUUUUUUUUUUUUUUU
```

4. IVO ABOVE CONTINGENCY PLANS MODIFIED TO HAVE NR1 SURFACE AND RETURN TO PORT SHOULD OPERATIONAL PRIORITIES NECESSITATE CONCURRENT OPS IN EASTERN SECTOR.

BT

UUUUUUUUUUUUUUUUUUUUUUUUUUUUUUUU   EXHIBIT A-8
U   U N C L A S S I F I E D   U
UUUUUUUUUUUUUUUUUUUUUUUUUUUUUUUU

ADMINISTRATIVE MESSAGE

ROUTINE

R041655Z JUN 86 ZYB

FM COMNAVSEASYSCOM WASHINGTON DC

TO CINCLANTFLT NORFOLK VA

INFO SECNAV WASHINGTON DC   CNO WASHINGTON DC
COMNAVSURFLANT NORFOLK VA   COMSUBLANT NORFOLK VA
COMSERVGRU TWO   COMSUBGRU TWO
COMSUBGRU SIX   COMSERVRON EIGHT
COMSUBRON TWO   COMSUBRON SIX
MOBDIVSALU TWO   COMEODGRU TWO
USS PRESERVER   USS OPPORTUNE
USS SUNBIRD   USS KITTIWAKE
SUBMARINE NR ONE

UNCLAS

SUBJ: SPACE SHUTTLE CHALLENGER SALVOPS

A. CNO WASHINGTON DC 312234Z JAN 86 (NOTAL)
B. COMNAVSEASYSCOM WASHINGTON DC 010155Z FEB 86 (NOTAL)
C. COMNAVSEASYSCOM WASHINGTON DC 061717Z FEB 86 (NOTAL)
D. COMNAVSEASYSCOM WASHINGTON DC 121809Z MAR 86 (NOTAL)
E. COMNAVSEASYSCOM WASHINGTON DC 212025Z MAR 86 (NOTAL)

1. PER REFS A THRU E CINCLANT FLT PROVIDED SEARCH AND RECOVERY ASSETS TO COMNAVSEA IN SUPPORT OF SPACE SHUTTLE CHALLENGER SALVOP DURING PERIOD 6 FEB THRU 1 JUN 86.

2. SCOPE OF THIS SALVOP WAS UNPARALLELED IN SEARCH AND RECOVERY ANNULS. OVER 480 SQ NM OF OCEAN BOTTOM WAS SEARCHED USING SIDE SCAN AND/OR CTFM SONAR AND 691 SONAR CONTACTS WERE IDENTIFIED, OF WHICH 491 WERE VISUALLY INVESTIGATED BY DIVERS, REMOTELY OPERATED VEHICLES (ROV'S), MANNED SUBMERSIBLES FOR SUBMARINE NR-1. OF THESE, 83 WERE CLASSIFIED AS SPACE SHUTTLE DEBRIS AND 62 OF HIGH INTEREST WERE SUCCESSFULLY RECOVERED. PRIMARY OBJECTIVES OF OPERATION WERE UNEQUIVOCALLY SATISFIED AS FOLLOWS:

00C(2)... ORIG FOR COMNAVSEASYSCOM WASH(8)   15710/15/0348
  00CS266(1) 00(1) 09(1) 08(1) PMS395(1) 09B4311(1)

                                                  RTD:120-000/COPIES:0008

016890/155   1 OF 2   MATA1214 155/23:47Z   041655Z JUN 86
CSN:VDTE00085   COMNAVSEASYCO

UUUUUUUUUUUUUUUUUUUUUUUUUUUUUUUU
U   U N C L A S S I F I E D   U
UUUUUUUUUUUUUUUUUUUUUUUUUUUUUUUU

UNCLASSIFIED

    A. BOTH UPPER AND LOWER SEGMENTS OF RIGHT SOLID ROCKET BOOSTER (SRB), POSITIVELY DISCLOSING A NOMINAL 28 IN. DIAMETER BURNTHROUGH AT FIELD JOINT IN QUESTION, WERE RECOVERED.
    B. REMAINS OF ALL SEVEN ASTRONAUTS WERE RECOVERED.
    C. MAJORITY OF CRITICAL ITEMS OF PAYLOAD WERE RECOVERED.
    D. ALL ITEMS OF INTEREST FROM ORBITER WERE RECOVERED.
3. FOL COMMANDS PROVIDED MAJOR ASSISTANCE TO SALVOP:
    A. USS PRESERVER (ARS 8)
    B. MOBILE DIVING AND SALVAGE UNIT TWO
    C. EXPLOSIVE ORDINANCE DISPOSAL GROUP TWO
    D. USS SUNBIRD (ASR 15)
    E. SUBMARINE NR-1
    F. USS OPPORTUNE (ARS 41)
    G. USS KITTIWAKE (ASR 13)
    H. RESCUE SALVAGE SHIP GRAPPLE

PARTICIPATING COMMANDS DEMONSTRATED PROFESSIONALISM AND TENACITY DEMANDED OF A COMPLEX SALVOP. THEIR DEDICATED SUPPORT WAS ESSENTIAL TO UNQUALIFIED SUCCESS OF CHALLENGER OP.

4. PERFORMANCE OF USS PRESERVER AND USS OPPORTUNE IN SPEARHEADING SHALLOW WATER DIVING/RECOVERY EFFORTS INVOLVING ORBITER/PAYLOAD AND USS SUNBIRD/NR-1 IN CLASSIFYING ALMOST 300 SONAR CONTACTS IN SRB HIGH INTEREST AREA IN LESS THAN TWO WEEKS IS PARTICULARLY NOTEWORTHY.

5. UNIT AWARD RECOMMENDATIONS WILL FOLLOW BY SEPCOR. VADM ROWDEN SENDS.

BT

EXHIBIT A-9

OFFICE OF THE DEPARTMENT OF DEFENSE MANAGER
SPACE TRANSPORTATION SYSTEM CONTINGENCY SUPPORT OPERATIONS
PETERSON AIR FORCE BASE, COLORADO 80914

3 DEC 1986

MEMORANDUM FOR THE CHIEF OF NAVAL OPERATIONS, DEPARTMENT OF THE NAVY, WASHINGTON, D.C. 20350

SUBJECT: STS Mission 51-L Challenger Salvage Operation Letter of Commendation

After the tragic loss of the Space Shuttle Challenger and crew on 28 January 1986, OOMS representatives at the Support Operations Center, Cape Canaveral AFS, Florida contacted the U.S. Navy Supervisor of Salvage within the Naval Sea Systems Command for search and salvage assistance. The Supervisor of Salvage personnel arrived at Cape Canaveral on 29 January to provide technical advice and begin operational planning. Assets were quickly identified and mobilized, the search area defined, and a side scan sonar search (which eventually covered more than 450 square nautical miles) was initiated.

Due to the urgency of the situation, Navy personnel from the Supervisor of Salvage office directed on-scene efforts of personnel and material assets from the Commander in Chief, U.S. Atlantic Fleet, the U.S. Air Force, the U.S. Coast Guard, NASA and numerous contractors employed under existing Navy and NASA contracts. Assets under direction of the Supervisor of Salvage included: four U.S. Navy ships, 11 other ships with unique capabilities, the research nuclear submarine (NR-1), manned submersibles, remotely operated vehicles, side scan sonars, towed metal detectors, and divers with a variety of specialized tools and equipment. Over 880 sonar contacts, some of which were debris fields, were detected and investigated. Eighty-nine percent (118 tons) of the 187 confirmed pieces of STS 51-L, were recovered from water depths ranging from 10 to 1200 feet. Despite the complexity of the effort, the environmental problems imposed by the Gulf Stream, and the necessity to coordinate sea operations and shore support for a fleet of vessels, the operation was totally successful.

The salvage of the wreckage from STS 51-L and the recovery of crew remains from Challenger were vitally important to the U.S. space program. Success of the operation was due in large measure to the outstanding support of the U.S. Navy. I extend my sincere appreciation to the U.S. Navy and commend the Supervisor of Salvage personnel for their selfless dedication to a joint services operation involving the support of thousands.

ROBERT T. HERRES
General, USAF
DOD Manager, STS Contingency
Support Operations

cc:
HQ NASA/Code A, Washington, D.C. 20546
SUPSALV, Washington, D.C. 20362-5101
ODMS, Patrick AFB, FL 32925-5675

ENCLOSURE (3)

Appendix B
MAJOR MOBILIZED ASSETS

SALVAGE SHIPS

PRESERVER (ARS 8)

Description: Rescue salvage ship (Naval Reserve Force)

Clear deck space 3,230 sq. ft.

Assets: GPS/LORAN C navigation system
Divers, videocameras, recompression chamber
Lifting capacity 10 tons FWD, 8 tons AFT

Primary Assignment/Operation: Shallow water search area (Orbiter)
Recovery operations

Period Employed: 8 February - 11 April 1986

Owner/Chartered: USN

SALVAGE SHIPS

OPPORTUNE (ARS 41)

Description: Rescue salvage ship

Clear deck space 3,440 square feet

Assets: ROV - SCORPI
GPS/LORAN C navigation system
Scan sonar, Mesotech sonar
Divers, videocamera, recompression chamber
Lifting capacity 20 tons FWD, 12 tons AFT

Primary Assignment/Operation: Shallow water search area (Orbiter)
Classification and recovery operations

Period Employed: 5 April - 1 June 1986

Owner/Chartered: USN

SALVAGE SHIPS

STENA WORKHORSE

Description: General purpose heavy work vessel

Clear deck space 6,030 sq. ft.

Assets: ROV - GEMINI
Dynamic positioning system
GPS/LORAN C navigation system
Helicopter, hospital, saturation diving system
100-ton lift capacity

Primary Assignment/Operation: Deep water search area (solid rocket booster) Recovery operations

Period Employed: 28 February - 1 May 1986

Owner/Chartered: Northern Coasters Ltd./Tracor Marine, Inc.

SUBMARINE RESCUE SHIPS

USS SUNBIRD (ASR 15)

Description: Submarine rescue ship

Clear deck space 3,440 sq. ft.

Assets: M.S. - NR-1
                  GPS/LORAN C navigation system
                  Scan sonar, Mesotech sonar
                  Divers, videocamera, recompression chamber
                  Lifting capacity 10 tons

Primary Assignment/Operation: Deep water search area (solid rocket booster)
                                  Classification and recovery operations

Period Employed: 20 February - 18 March 1986
                  31 March - 17 April 1986

Owner/Chartered: USN

SUBMARINE RESCUE SHIPS

USS KITTIWAKE (ASR 13)

Description: Submarine rescue ship

Clear deck space 3,440 square feet

Assets: Divers, recompression chamber
Lifting capacity 10 tons

Primary Assignment/Operation: Recovery operations, dive platform

Period Employed: 11 April - 22 April 1986

Owner/Chartered: USN

SUBMARINES

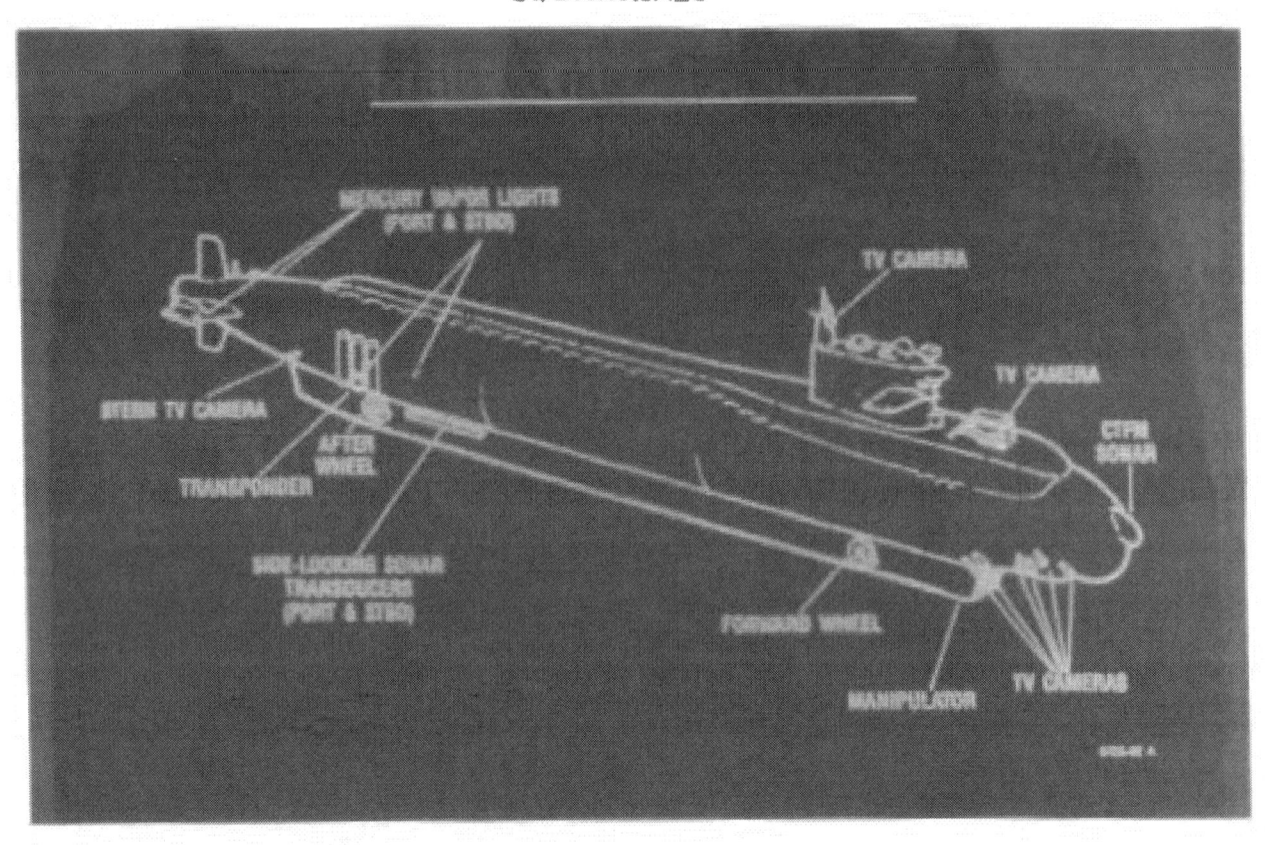

NUCLEAR RESEARCH 1 (NR-1)

Description: Nuclear research submarine with seven-man crew

Operating depth to 2,375 feet

Assets: Computer dead reckoning navigation system
SIDE/LOOK R2400 sonar
SIDE/LOOK R600 sonar
FWD (3) R1500
FWD (1) R90
11 video cameras, 4 still cameras, 2 sample collection baskets, 4 deployable transponders
Lifting capacity 500-1,000 lbs.

Primary Assignment/Operation: Search and classification

Period Employed: 20 February - 18 March 1988
31 March - 17 April 1988

Owner/Chartered: USN

SEARCH VESSELS

LCU (CHS-1925)

Description: USAF Range search and salvage vessel

Assets: LORAC (A)
Scan sonar, Megotech sonar
Divers
Clear deck space 1,400 sq. ft.
Lifting capacity 10 tons

Primary Assignment/Operation: Shallow water search area (Orbiter)
Search, classification and recovery

Period Employed: 8 February - 7 April 1986

Owner/Chartered: USAF/NASA

SEARCH VESSELS

FREEDOM STAR

Description: SRB surface retrieval vessel

Clear deck space 2,420 sq. ft.

Assets: Stern thrust positioning system
            GPS/LORAN C navigation system
            Divers, metal detector, recompression chamber

Primary Assignment/Operation: Shallow water search area (Orbiter)
                                  Search operations

Period Employed: 8 February - 2 May 1986

Owner/Chartered: NASA/Morton Thiokol, Inc.

SEARCH VESSELS

G.W. PIERCE II

Description: General purpose work vessel

Clear deck space 2,390 sq. ft.

Assets: GPS/LORAN C side scan sonar
Divers, videocamera
Lifting capacity 12.5 tons

Primary Assignment/Operation: Deep water search area (solid rocket booster)
Search operations

Period Employed: 25 February - 1 April 1986

Owner/Chartered: Tracor Marine, Inc.

SEARCH VESSELS

PAUL LANGEVIN III

Description: General purpose work vessel

Clear deck space 2,600 sq. ft.

Assets: GPS/LORAN C navigation system
          Side scan sonar
          Towed metal detector
          Lifting capacity 10 tons

Primary Assignment/Operation: Shallow water search area (Orbiter)
                                Search operations

Period Employed: 13 February - 15 August 1986

Owner/Chartered: Tracor Marine, Inc.

SEARCH VESSELS

LIBERTY STAR

Description: SRB surface retrieval vessel

Clear deck space 2,420 sq. ft.

Assets: Side scan sonar
                 GPS/LORAN C navigation system
                 Stern thrust positioning system
                 Divers, metal detectors, towed metal detector

Primary Assignment/Operation: Deep water search area (solid rocket booster)
                                Search operations

Period Employed: 8 February - 22 June 86
                   23 June - 29 August 86

Owner/Chartered: NASA/Morton Thiokol, Inc.

SUPPORT VESSELS

INDEPENDENCE

Description: SRB surface retrieval vessel

Clear deck space 4,200 sq. ft., lifting capacity 4.5 tons

Assets: ROV's - Deep Drone, ASD 620, SCORPI
Bow & stern thruster positioning system
GPS/LORAN C TRISPONDER navigation system
Divers, metal detectors, recompression chamber

Primary Assignment/Operation: Shallow water search area (Orbiter)
Classification Operations

Period Employed: 8 February - 29 August 1986

Owner/Chartered: USAF/NASA/Morton Thiokol, Inc.

SUPPORT VESSELS

R/V SEWARD JOHNSON

Description: A 176-foot boat designed specifically for oceanographic research and as a mothership for transporting and launching both Johnson SEA-LINK 4-man submersibles

Assets: Worked with SEA-LINK II
360 DEG, Thrusters stabilization system
GPS/LORAN C positioning system
Dry lab and wet lab
Clear deck space 3,120
Lifting capacity 5 tons, Sub (18), Bow & Stern

Primary Assignment/Operation: Deep water search area (solid rocket booster) Classification and recovery operations

Period Employed: 21 February - 19 April 1986

Owner/Chartered: Harbor Branch/Eastport International, Inc.

SUPPORT VESSELS

R/V EDWIN LINK

Description: A 123-foot converted Coast Guard cutter used to deploy and recover submersibles

Assets: Worked with SEA-LINK I
Bow thruster positioning-stabilization system
Decompression facilities
Clear deck space 1,440
Lifting capacity 5 tons. Sub (12)

Primary Assignment/Operation: Deep water search area (solid rocket booster)
Classification and recovery operations

Period Employed: 27 March - 1 May 1986

Owner/Chartered: Harbor Branch/Eastport International, Inc.

SUPPORT VESSELS

F/V BIG FOOT

Description: A 90-foot scallop fishing boat used for dredging the ocean bottom in shallow water areas

Assets: Dual hauling booms
Warping Winch
Shellfish Modified Bottom Trawl Net

Primary Assignment/Operation: Shallow water search area (Orbiter)
Recovery operations (dredging)

Period Employed: 5 April 1986

Owner/Chartered: Port Canaveral Seafood Company/Tracor Marine, Inc.

LOGISTIC VESSELS

ELIMINATOR

Description: Charter fishing boat

Assets: LORAN C navigation system

Primary Assignment/Operation: Logistic support, personnel and cargo transfer

Period Employed: 23 February - 26 June 1986

Owner/Chartered: Private/Tracor Marine, Inc.

LOGISTIC VESSELS

PELICAN PRINCESS

Description: Charter fishing boat

Assets: LORAN C navigation system

Primary Assignment/Operation: Logistic support, personnel and cargo transfer

Period Employed: 17 February - 24 February 1986

Owner/Chartered: Private/Tracor Marine, Inc.

SUBMERSIBLES

JOHNSON SEA-LINK I AND II

Description: Manned submersibles designed for deep diving in depths to 2,640 feet

Assets: Visual navigation system
Scan sonar
Still and high resolution television cameras
One 7-function manipulator arm

Primary Assignment/Operation: Classification and recovery

Period Employed: 27 March - 1 May 1986

Owner/Chartered: Harbor Branch/Eastport International, Inc.

REMOTELY OPERATED VEHICLES

GEMINI

Description: A remotely operated, open frame highly adaptable subsea work system (depths to 10,000 feet)

Assets: Seven hydraulic thrusters positioning system
Tether management assembly
Scan sonar, 255 CTFM sonar
Three television cameras, three still cameras
Lifting capacity 1,500 lbs.
Two RSI 7.5 function manipulators

Primary Assignment/Operation: Classification and recovery

Period Employed: 28 February - 1 May 1986

Owner/Chartered: Eastport International, Inc.

REMOTELY OPERATED VEHICLES

DEEP DRONE

Description: State of the art tethered unmanned vehicle designed to perform search and salvage to 6000 feet

Assets: Three 5 horsepower electric thrusters
Two 2.5 horsepower hydraulic thrusters
Umbilical positioning system
CTFM sonar
Three videocameras, one 35 mm still camera
Two hydraulic manipulators, one 5-function unit and one 7-function unit

Primary Assignment/Operation: Classification and recovery

Period Employed: 8 February - 26 April 1986

Owner/Chartered: USN/Eastport International, Inc.

REMOTELY OPERATED VEHICLES

SCORPI

Description: A versatile and reliable remotely operated underwater work system designed primarily for inspection and non-destructive testing at depths to 3,000 feet

Assets: 5 hyd. thrusters
Umbilical positioning system
250 CTFM sonar
Two videocameras, one 35 mm still camera
Lifting capacity 110 lbs.

Primary Assignment/Operation: Classification and recovery

Period Employed: 22 April - 6 July 1986

Owner/Chartered: Eastport International, Inc.

REMOTELY OPERATED VEHICLES

ASD 620

Description: A remotely operated vehicle used for underwater inspection and work

Assets: 7 hyd. thrusters, umbilical positioning system
250 CTFM sonar
One video, one 35 mm still camera
MERPRO 3-function manipulator
Lifting capacity 110 pounds

Primary Assignment/Operation: Classification and recovery

Period Employed: 11 May - 8 June 1986

Owner/Chartered: Eastport International, Inc.

Appendix C
CONTACTS RECOVERED

Summary of Underwater STS 51-L Contacts Recovered

System: Right SRB

Contact Number	Remarks
0021	Aft Segment Skirt
0131	Aft Center Segment w/Burn Area
0195	Forward Aft Center Segment
0292	Forward Aft Segment
0301	Aft Forward Segment
0325	Aft Center Segment
0433	Aft Center Segment
0502	Forward Center Segment
0538	Forward Skirt and Parachute
0579	Aft Segment
0615	Forward Center Segment
0699	Forward Segment
0712	Aft Segment w/Burn Area

System: Orbiter

Contact Number	Remarks
0008	Hydraulic Lines
0010	Engine Parts
0023	Engine Parts
0030	3' Cable Tray Exit
0066	Main Orbiter Engine Nozzle
0067	Crew Compartment
0068	Aft Fuselage
0071	Miscellaneous Small Hardware
0072	Miscellaneous Medium Hardware
0077	Medium Sidewall Piece
0078	Medium Cone Shape
0192	Large Hydrazine Tank
0520	Left Aft Fuselage
0527	AC Motor
0527A	Aileron
0530	Vertical Stabilizer
0547	Miscellaneous Medium Hardware
0555	External Large Piece
0558	Engine Nozzle
0563	Avionics Box
0563A	Miscellaneous Small Pieces
0564	Aft Cargo Hold
0565	Aft Fuselage and Tank
0566	Right Wing

Summary of Underwater STS 51-L Contacts Recovered (Con't.)

System: Orbiter (continued)

Contact Number	Remarks
0567	Electronics and Wiring
0568	Left Fuselage Sidewall
0571	Large Right Side Piece
0571A	Large Piece
0571B	Large Pieces (2)
0572	External Medium Piece
0595	Large Left Wing Piece
****	Crew Compartment
****	Orbiter Cargo
****	Orbiter Cargo
0716	Small External Piece
0723	Large Piece, Metal and Velcro
0729	Large External Piece
0752	Wiring/Piping/Tiles
0754	Medium Piece and Tiles, Wiring
0757	Cargo Bay Door Hinge Assembly
0765	Large Piece
0766	Cargo Bay Door Assembly
0767	Medium Piece, Aft Orbiter
0768	Actuator, Cargo Bay
0772	Medium Piece Structure/Spartan Halley
0776	Medium Piece
0777	Medium Piece, Cargo Bay
0778	Large Piece
0779	Medium Piece, Aft Bulkhead of Cargo Bay
0780	Large Piece, Orbiter Sidewall
0781	Small Metal Piece
0782	Medium Piece, Fuselage
0783	Medium Piece
0784	Medium Piece, Flat Piping
0786	Large Piece, ET Attachment and Fuselage
0790	Electronics, Cargo Bay Aft
0793	Medium Piece, A-Frame w/Tiles
0795	Medium Pieces (2), Tiles and Forward Landing Gear
0796	Medium Pieces (3), Cargo Bay Keel Bridges
0798	Medium Pieces (3), Pipes, Valves and OMES Pod
0803	Medium Piece, External w/Tiles
0805	Medium Piece
0806	Medium Pieces (3), Left Wing, Wall, Mid-Body
0808	Small Piece, Cargo Bay Door
0808A	Medium Pieces (2), Internal
0809	Medium Pieces (14), Miscellaneous
0811	Large Pieces (2), Left Fuselage and Cargo Bay Door
0814	Large Piece, Orbiter to ET Attachment
0816	Large Piece, Right Fuselage, Cargo Bay Door

Summary of Underwater STS 51-L Contacts Recovered (Con't.)

System: Orbiter (continued)

Contact Number	Remarks
0818	Medium Metal Piece
0819	Medium Piece, Valve Panel
0825	Medium Piece, Aft Sidewall, Cargo Bay
0826	Medium Piece, Aft OMS Pod Deck
0827	Medium Piece, Cargo Bay Door
0829	Medium Piece, Left Wing
0830	4' Diameter Tank, PRSD
0833	Medium Piece, LOX Feed Line
0834	Medium Piece, Cargo Bay Door
0836	18" Hydrazine Reservoir
0837	Medium Piece, Aft Sidewall
0838	Medium Piece, Hatch, Cargo Bay Side
0839	Medium Pieces (2), External
0840	Medium Piece, OMS Pod
0843	Medium Piece, Manipulator Arm
0846	Medium Metal Piece
0849	Small Metal Piece
0850	Large External Piece
0857	Medium Piece, Thruster, 3 Ports
0858	Small Metal Piece w/5-Boxes
0861	Small Metal Drum w/Motor
0864	Small Manifold Board w/6-Actuators
0865	Small Metal Piece, Forward Cargo Bay
0866	Small Pieces (3) w/Hydraulic Fittings and Valves
0867	Small Piece, Payload Thrusters (2)
0868	Small Piece
0869	Small Piece, Actuator Motor w/Valve
0870	Small Piece w/Wiring
0871	Small Wiring Bundle
0871A	Medium Pieces (3), Strut
0872	Small Metal Piece
0873	Small Metal Piece
0876	Small Metal Pieces (4) w/Hydraulic Lines
0877	Small Metal Pieces (2), w/Tile, Wiring
0879	Medium Metal Piece w/Tile
0880	Medium Piece, Corrugated Metal
0883	Small Metal Piece
0884	Medium Sized Tank
0885	Small Metal Piece w/Tile

Summary of Underwater STS 51-L Contacts Recovered (Con't.)

System: Left SRB

Contact Number	Remarks
0011	Forward Aft Segment
0026	Forward AFt Center Segment
0196	External Tank Attachment w/Clevis
0635	Forward Motor Casing
5124	SRB External Tank Strut

System: External Tank

Contact Number	Remarks
0003	External Small Pieces
0004	External Medium Piece
0029	External Large Piece
0183	External Medium Piece
0560	External Large Piece
0562	External Large Piece
0724	Large ET Piece w/Strainer
0758	Large ET Piece w/Feedline
0762	Medium Metal Picce
0763	External Medium Piece
0769	External Large Piece
0787	External Large Piece
0788	Large Piece, Hydrogen Tank
0810	External Large Piece, Hydrogen Tank
0815	Medium Piece, LOX Internal Tank
0824	Large Piece, LOX Feed Line
0862	External Large Piece
0863	External Large Piece w/Stiffener Ring

System: Booster, Unknown Side

Contact Number	Remarks
0214	Large Curved External Piece
0312	Large External Piece
0468	Large External Piece
0487	Large External Piece w/Clevis
0510	Large External Piece
0524	Large External Piece
0605	Medium External Piece

Summary of Underwater STS 51-L Contacts Recovered (Concluded)

System: Booster, Unknown Side (continued)

Contact Number	Remarks
0631	Medium External Piece w/Clevis and Tang
0711	Medium External Piece
0538	Large External Piece w/Clevis
0539	Large External Piece w/Tang
5125	Medium External Piece
5126	Medium External Pieces (3)
5127	Large External/Internal Piece
5128	Medium External Piece
5433	Medium Motor Skin Piece

System: Shuttle, Unknown

Contact Number	Remarks
0547	Medium Pieces (2)
0728	Small Valves